American History: A Very Short Introduction

VERY SHORT INTRODUCTIONS are for anyone wanting a stimulating and accessible way in to a new subject. They are written by experts and have been published in more than 25 languages worldwide.

The series began in 1995 and now represents a wide variety of topics in history, philosophy, religion, science, and the humanities. The VSI library now contains more than 300 volumes—a Very Short Introduction to everything from ancient Egypt and Indian philosophy to conceptual art and cosmology—and will continue to grow in a variety of disciplines.

Very Short Introductions available now:

Available soon:

For more information visit our web site

www.oup.co.uk/general/vsi/

Paul S. Boyer

AMERICAN HISTORY

A Very Short Introduction

OXFORD
UNIVERSITY PRESS

OXFORD
UNIVERSITY PRESS

Oxford University Press, Inc., publishes works that further
Oxford University's objective of excellence
in research, scholarship, and education.

Oxford   New York
Auckland   Cape Town   Dar es Salaam   Hong Kong   Karachi
Kuala Lumpur   Madrid   Melbourne   Mexico City   Nairobi
New Delhi   Shanghai   Taipei   Toronto

With offices in
Argentina   Austria   Brazil   Chile   Czech Republic   France   Greece
Guatemala   Hungary   Italy   Japan   Poland   Portugal   Singapore
South Korea   Switzerland   Thailand   Turkey   Ukraine   Vietnam

Published by Oxford University Press, Inc.
198 Madison Avenue, New York, NY 10016

www.oup.com

Oxford is a registered trademark of Oxford University Press

Library of Congress Cataloging-in-Publication Data
Boyer, Paul S.
American history : a very short introduction / Paul S. Boyer.
p.   cm. — (Very short introductions)
Includes bibliographical references and index.
ISBN 978-0-19-538914-2 (pbk.)
1. United States—History. I. Title.
E178.B782   2012
973—dc23   2012004837

7 9 8 6

Printed in Great Britain
by Ashford Colour Press Ltd., Gosport, Hants.
on acid-free paper

I lovingly dedicate this work to my dear wife, Ann Chapman Boyer, who has been a pillar of strength in many ways during its completion, and also to our son, Alex, and his wife, Mary, and our daughter, Kate, and her husband, Michael, for their unstinting love and support. I also dedicate the book to our grandsons, Ethan and Jake, hoping it may pique their interest in the field to which their grandfather devoted his career.

Contents

List of illustrations

Preface

Of the many challenges confronting anyone rash enough to set
about writing an American history, perhaps the most formidable
is simply to penetrate the dense clouds of myth, preconceptions,
and ideological abstractions that sometimes seem to envelop
the nation's history so completely that the unadorned reality
disappears in the mists. From the earliest European discoveries of
the lands that lay westward across the Atlantic, writers invested
them with hopes, dreams, and wild imaginings. Although these
vast continents were home to several million human beings and
complex societies, Europeans envisioned them as enticingly empty
and full of promise—literally a "New World." In a book published
in 1516, twenty-four years after Christopher Columbus made
landfall in the Caribbean, the English philosopher and statesman
Thomas More imagined an ideal society, which he called "Utopia,"
situated on an island off present-day Brazil. In More's fictional
New World, harmony, cooperation, and equality prevail; property
is held in common; and the lust for gold is unknown. (In a nice
touch, chamber pots in More's Utopia are made of gold—evidence
of the prevailing contempt for the worthless metal.)

Centuries later, as tidal waves of immigrants poured into the
United States, many carried in their mental baggage fond images
of the promise of their future homeland, symbolized by the Statue

of Liberty in New York harbor. The 1883 poem by Emma Lazarus
that is inscribed on its base ends:

> Give me your tired, your poor, your huddled masses,
> Yearning to breathe free,
> The wretched refuse of your teeming shore,
> Send these, the homeless, tempest-tost to me,
> I lift my lamp beside the golden door!

For some, the dream came true; for others, it collapsed in bitter
disappointment. For most, everyday reality, with its mix of
achievements and setbacks, soon replaced idealized fantasies. (For
the millions of enslaved Africans transported to the Americas by
force, no preconceived illusions intruded on the grim reality of
their immigrant experience.)

Others invested the New World with religious significance.
Columbus became convinced in his later years that God had
guided his voyages of discovery, fulfilling biblical prophecies of
a future millennial age. Much later, the New England Puritans
drew inspiration from the conviction that America would play
a key role in an unfolding divine plan culminating in Christ's
earthly kingdom. Even today, many American evangelical believers
continue to envision a special place for the nation in God's cosmic
scheme—or sadly conclude that the United States, corrupted by
worldly pursuits, has forfeited the divine favor it once enjoyed.

In semi-secularized form, notions of American exceptionalism
seeped into the work of historians and textbook writers who
presented highly selective versions of the nation's history as a
story of freedom, opportunity, and endless progress, blessedly
free of the dark and exploitive features that defaced less-favored
societies. Such self-serving interpretations gradually faded
under the battering of events and the leaching of supernaturalist
assumptions from historical scholarship. Yet as recently as the
1980s, President Ronald Reagan could still inspire many as he

evoked ancient images of America as "a shining city on a hill" enjoying a uniquely favored destiny.

For others, abstract conceptions of "America" and its meaning took more sinister forms. For Marxist ideologues and vociferous opponents of neo-colonialism and economic imperialism, the United States stands as the epitome of late capitalism, extending its corporate tentacles everywhere in the search for markets, cheap labor, and natural resources. Still others, treasuring indigenous folkways and regional cultures, have denounced America as the source of a debased and corrupting global mass culture. While not without merit, such stereotypes hardly convey the full story. For Islamist revolutionaries, gripped by the vision of a worldwide righteous order willed by Allah and set forth in the Qu'ran, the United States looms as a massive impediment, the Great Satan, blocking fulfillment of the dream.

These varied mythologies, idealized abstractions, and ideological constructs, while fascinating to historians of ideas, stand in the way of understanding America's actual history, stripped of preconceptions or extraneous agendas. Perfect objectivity is another illusion, of course, yet it remains a worthwhile goal. The reader will not find in these pages one over-arching procrustean interpretive thesis into which everything is forced to fit. Certain broad realities will structure much of the narrative—immigration, urbanization, slavery, continental expansion; the global projection of U.S. power, the centrality of religion, the progression from an agrarian to an industrial to a post-industrial economic order. Yet in delineating such large themes, the work also acknowledges the diversity of the American experience; the importance of individual actors; and the crucial role of race, ethnicity, gender, and social class in shaping the experience of specific groups within the larger tapestry of the nation's history.

This brief introduction to the vast topic of U.S. history avoids either an excessively upbeat, rose-tinted approach or an unduly negative one. To be sure, from a contemporary perspective, much in American history—like much in the history of many nations—tempts one to censure and moralizing judgment. The gap between historical reality and the lofty rhetoric of chauvinists, politicians, and flag-waving patriots even invites ridicule and irony. Yet such a stance involves its own distortions. Throughout, the aim has been to present the story in a critical yet balanced and reasonably non-ideological fashion, mostly leaving it to the reader to make such judgments as seem warranted. American history is the story of one society among many, distinctive in some ways, yet sharing in the common human condition. It comprises one brief, unfinished chapter in the great volume of world history, the cumulative record of what the philosopher Immanuel Kant called "the crooked timber of humanity." This small book makes no pretense of being final or definitive. It represents the best efforts of one observer, himself a product of the society and a citizen of the nation whose history he is recording.

Anyone who undertakes a *brief* history of America, one that can be read in a single sitting, faces additional challenges. Much must be omitted, anecdotal digressions regretfully bypassed, and corroborating evidence for broad generalizations left to bulkier studies. Yet the discipline of brevity has its advantages. Such a concise format forces one to make tough judgments about what was truly significant, to focus on the main threads of the story, and to pinpoint the key turning points and themes of lasting significance. And this format also places a premium on clarity and readability, in fairness to readers willing to spend a few hours in the company of an unknown author. I hope this work at least in part meets these multiple challenges.

Madison, Wisconsin
January 2012

Acknowledgments

First and foremost I acknowledge Nancy Toff, editor extraordinaire at Oxford University Press, who invited me to undertake this challenging project, encouraged me at every stage, and provided exceptional support toward the end as medical concerns threatened to distract my attention. Sonia Tycko processed the chapters with exemplary efficiency, Emily Sacharin traced references with amazing skill, Joellyn Ausanka carried the project through the demanding production process, and Mary Sutherland did the copyediting beautifully. By good fortune, my sister-in-law, Marion Talbot Brady, a gifted copyeditor of many years' experience, happened to be visiting just as the final proofreading was under way and generously provided assistance in completing the project. My thanks to all.

Beyond these immediate debts, I owe sincere thanks to the vast host of historians (some listed in the Further reading section) on whose scholarly work I have relied in preparing this introduction to the vast topic of American history. I hope that readers of this work will be inspired to turn to that great body of work for deeper analyses of the topics and themes briefly treated in this very short introduction.

Chapter 1
Beginnings: Pre-history to 1763

Contemporary Americans, immersed in the busy rhythms of twenty-first-century life, rarely pause to reflect that they dwell in a land that has been inhabited for millennia. Human settlement on the continent we call North America (after the Florentine cartographer Amerigo Vespucci) began at least 15,000 years ago, as bands of people in present-day Siberia came by water or across a now-vanished land bridge into today's Alaska. As migration continued and numbers increased, these first Americans spread southward and eastward, encountering regions of widely divergent climate and topography. Distinctive groups with differing languages, social organization, religious practices, and sources of livelihood gradually evolved.

In present-day New Mexico, one group, the Anasazi, built settlements called pueblos, crafted jewelry and decorated pottery, and wrested a living from the arid soil. Farther east, a major civilization arose at Cahokia (today's East St. Louis), where the Mississippi and Missouri Rivers converge. Along the Atlantic Coast, other groups, or tribes, engaged in hunting, farming, and fishing. They established diplomatic relations, occasionally fought wars, and maintained extensive trading networks. In today's upstate New York, leaders of five large tribes came together sometime after 1450 to form an alliance, the Iroquois Federation. On the western plains, around the

Great Lakes, and in today's upper Midwest other groups pursued agriculture, fishing, and buffalo hunting, depending on their region's ecology.

By 1500, the North American population comprised an estimated seven to ten million people. Millions more lived in Mesoamerica and South America, where a series of civilizations—Mayan, Aztec, and the still-expanding Incan empire—had flourished for more than a millennium.

These civilizations remained unknown in Europe. Leif Erikson and other Norse voyagers had reached the northeastern tip of North America as early as 1000, and even established a short-lived settlement in Newfoundland. But apart from such isolated contacts, the peoples of the Americas and Europe knew nothing of each other's existence. This would soon change, however, with momentous implications for both.

1. Cliff dwellings at Mesa Verde National Park, Colorado. Built by ancient pre-Columbian settlers of North America, these complex settlements were abandoned in the twelfth and thirteenth centuries as rainfall failed.

The age of European exploration

Late fifteenth-century Europe seethed with intellectual ferment, technological innovations, and economic changes. Seeking faster trading routes to Asia, Portuguese navigators ventured around the tip of Africa and on eastward to India. Others contemplated an even more daring route—westward across the Atlantic. One of these, the Italian Christopher Columbus, persuaded the Spanish monarchs Ferdinand and Isabella to finance a voyage. Miscalculating the size of the earth and blissfully unaware that vast continents lay in the way, Columbus—on August 3, 1492—set out from Palos, Spain, with a three-ship flotilla, bound for Asia. Instead, he made landfall on October 12 on an island he called San Salvador. Still convinced that he had found "the Indies," he called the local islanders "Indians"—and the name stuck.

A tangle of economic, political, and religious motives drove this exploratory fever. Columbus himself (who made three subsequent voyages) was gripped by ambitions for wealth and honors, and zeal to convert the Indians to Christianity. He also saw his voyages as fulfillments of biblical prophecies—an early instance of a persistent tendency to view America as the object of God's special interest. The monarchs who financed these probes into the unknown sought to extend their domains, outshine their rivals, and acquire the fabulous riches that many believed abounded in what Shakespeare in *The Tempest* called this "brave new world."

The spread of European settlements

The watery trail blazed by Columbus soon became heavily traveled as Europe's seagoing powers staked their claims. Spanish settlements in present-day Florida (St. Augustine, 1565) and New Mexico (Santa Fe, 1609), as well as in the Caribbean, Mexico, and Central and South America, brought a tide of Spanish-speaking soldiers, adventurers, colonial administrators, and Catholic missionaries.

The Dutch soon followed. In 1609 Henry Hudson, an English navigator employed by the Dutch East India Company, sailed up the river that now bears his name. In 1625 the Dutch East India Company established Nieuw Amsterdam on Manhattan Island, purchased from the local Lenape Indians. The company granted lands along the Hudson to proprietors, called patroons, who extracted taxes and fees from the tenant farmers who settled the region.

The English came late to this race for empire but soon made up for lost time. The Protestant Reformation that reached England in the 1530s gave England's American colonies, except for Maryland, a strongly Protestant cast. (Maryland, established in 1632 by Cecilius Calvert, a Catholic, on a grant from Charles I, sheltered English Catholics fleeing persecution at home.)

England's first permanent foothold in North America lay in a region that the English called Virginia, after Elizabeth I, the Virgin Queen. In 1607 a motley group of some six hundred settlers, financed by a company of investors called "adventurers," reached Virginia and built a fort, Jamestown, named for Elizabeth's successor, James I. The adventurers' hopes for riches from gold and silver faded fast, and disease, starvation, and Indian attacks soon carried off most of the initial settlers. However, tobacco, first cultivated in Virginia in 1611, became a profitable export as a pipe-smoking vogue swept Europe. In a 1604 pamphlet James I had denounced tobacco as "loathsome to the eye, hateful to the Nose, harmfull to the braine, [and] dangerous to the Lungs," but to little effect.

More English colonies spread southward—from North and South Carolina to Georgia—eventually encountering Spain's outpost in Florida. Tobacco reigned supreme in these southern colonies, supplemented by rice and indigo. The Protestant Church of England drew the most adherents, but the region's religious mosaic also included Scottish Presbyterians who favored more

4

decentralized church governance; Quakers espousing simple living and Christ's guidance, or "inner light," within each individual; and Methodists and Baptists preaching personal conversation and heartfelt religion over forms and rituals.

Farther north, in present-day Massachusetts, a small company of English religious dissenters who had wholly separated from the Church of England planted a settlement, called Plymouth, in 1620. These "Pilgrims," as they became known, arrived from Holland, where they had been living in exile. In 1621 they held a harvest feast, shared with local Wampanoag Indians, which evolved into a major American holiday, Thanksgiving. A history of the settlement by the first governor, William Bradford, written in simple, unadorned prose, ranks as an early classic of American literature.

The larger, more historically significant Massachusetts Bay colony was established at Boston in 1630. The founders were not Separatists, but "Puritans," so called because they desired to purify the Church of England of surviving popish practices. Later caricatured as joyless prudes, the Puritans were mainly distinguished by a set of ecclesiastical beliefs: worship should be austere and Bible based, church and civil authority wholly distinct, each congregation autonomous and self-governing, and church membership restricted to persons who could attest to a personal conversion experience.

After initial struggles, New Englanders prospered, achieving high levels of health and longevity. Settlements spread south to Rhode Island and Connecticut and north to New Hampshire, Vermont, and Maine. Along with farming, fisheries, and urban occupations, they conducted oceangoing trade. Carrying timber, grain, naval stores, and dried codfish to England and England's island colonies in the West Indies, these New England ships brought sugar and molasses (mainly for distilling into rum) from the West Indies and tea, furniture, dishware, and other manufactured goods from England itself.

In the Middle Atlantic region, Pennsylvania, New York, Delaware, and New Jersey rounded out England's North American colonies. In 1681 Charles II granted a charter to William Penn, the son of a naval admiral who in 1660 had helped restore the English monarchy after years of civil war. This charter granted young Penn sweeping powers to establish and govern a new colony. A Quaker convert, Penn considered his namesake province a "Holy Experiment." Under his leadership, Pennsylvania welcomed persecuted English Quakers as well as European religious dissenters, including Swiss and German Mennonites.

In 1664, amid a broader imperial conflict between England and the Netherlands, Nieuw Amsterdam's governor surrendered to an occupying English force. Renamed New York (after the Duke of York, the future King James II), the colony became a thriving, ethnically diverse commercial center with a fertile agricultural hinterland in the Hudson Valley. As the Dutch patroons gradually lost power, individual farm ownership on the New England model became the rule.

Delaware, originally a Swedish fur-trading post, passed to New Netherlands and then to the English. New Jersey, carved out of New York by James II and granted to a contentious group of proprietors, became a royal province in 1702.

Natives and newcomers: a fateful encounter

American historians once self-servingly mythologized pre-Columbian America as a "virgin land," a virtually empty wilderness. In fact, the European colonizers confronted extensive, complex, and long-established native societies. With profound implications for both newcomers and natives, this encounter took varied forms, from negotiations, trade, and strategic alliances to bloody conflict, new diseases (smallpox devastated Indian communities, which had no immunity), and misunderstandings arising from differing cosmologies and social systems.

In the Spanish colonies, missionaries and secular administrators viewed the natives as laborers, potential converts, and, sometimes, deadly foes. A 1680 Pueblo and Apache uprising left some four hundred Spanish officials and priests dead. Twelve years later, the Spanish reasserted control. Christopher Columbus himself established the template for the newcomers' view of the aboriginal population. "They ought to make good and skilled servants," he wrote; "I think they can very easily be made Christians. . . . I could conquer the whole of them with 50 men, and govern them as I please."

In English settlements, relations were at times reasonably harmonious. Sometimes colonists and Indians joined forces against a common enemy. In Connecticut in 1637, for example, the colonists allied with local Mohegans and Narragansetts against the Pequots. During this operation, Connecticut militiamen burned a Pequot village and slaughtered several hundred men, women, and children who were desperately trying to escape.

Relations often turned exploitive and violent, a situation exacerbated by differing views of property rights. To native peoples, the land was for use and could be shared. Europeans viewed land ownership as contractual and exclusive. From these differences, and the colonists' inexorable expansion onto native lands, sprang bitter conflicts. In Jamestown, a 1622 uprising by the local Powhatan Indians decimated the settlement. In 1763 Scots Irish settlers along the Susquehanna River, accusing Pennsylvania's Quaker leaders of neglecting frontier security, slaughtered and scalped peaceful Conestoga Indians in nearby villages.

In New England, simmering tensions exploded in 1675–76 as the Wampanoag sachem Metacom declared war against the ever-encroaching newcomers. Indians struck across the frontier, killing some 2,500 settlers. The colonists retaliated with equal ferocity, killing many Indians and selling prisoners into slavery.

When Metacom was captured, colonists displayed his severed head as a grim trophy of war.

The colonial period, in short, began a tragically persistent pattern of native peoples decimated by conflict, new diseases, and the relentless advance of white settlements. By 1800 the U.S. Indian population stood at about 600,000, a pathetic remnant of the estimated 2.2 million on the eve of European colonization.

Slavery takes root in America

This era also saw the introduction of slavery, planting the seeds of civil war and a noxious harvest of racism. Prevalent in ancient civilizations, slavery had long flourished in Africa and the Arab world. Now, like a spreading virus, it crossed the Atlantic.

The first slave ship arrived in Jamestown in 1619, and many more followed. Initially, Africans blended into a larger population of unfree laborers, including white indentured servants, who worked for a contracted period of time for employers who paid their passage to America. But as indentured servants fulfilled their obligations, they and their descendants entered the free labor force. Africans, by contrast, cultural and ethnic outsiders, their dark skin signifying their unfree status, became a permanently enslaved class. A 1705 Virginia law defined slavery as a perpetual condition, transmitted through the mother (thereby including the offspring of white masters and female slaves).

From small beginnings, slavery spread into the Spanish and Portuguese colonies, and England's colonies in the West Indies and North America. British slave ships dominated this human traffic, but New England ship owners participated as well. By 1790 the number of enslaved persons in North America—concentrated in the tobacco and rice colonies of Virginia, Maryland, and farther south but present throughout the colonies—stood at some 700,000.

Periodic slave uprisings—in New York in 1712, South Carolina in 1739—were brutally suppressed. Isolated moral protests by some New Englanders and Pennsylvania Quakers and Mennonites accomplished little. Woven into colonial society and economic life, slavery would survive into the 1860s, and its aftereffects far beyond.

A new society takes shape

In popular memory, and in the textbooks of earlier times, the nearly three hundred years of American history from 1492 to 1776 flicker randomly in disjointed, semi-mythic images: a beautiful Indian princess saving John Smith's life in Jamestown, resolute Pilgrims stepping ashore onto Plymouth Rock, the Dutch buying Manhattan Island for a few trinkets, accused witches hanged in Salem, romantic Spanish missions in California.

Yet this era gave rise to social patterns and modes of perception that would long endure. In addition to the fraught interactions of European settlers, native peoples, and enslaved Africans, other colonial-era realities had crucial long-term implications.

Long before the Declaration of Independence, England's American colonies experienced de facto independence, enjoying a measure of self-governance and economic autonomy. While the British government claimed ultimate power, in actual practice the colonies increasingly managed their own affairs. As they did, many colonists scarcely thought of themselves as British subjects, and chafed under the authority and deference claimed by officials dispatched from London.

Similarly, colonists increasingly saw their economic interests in local terms rather than through the lens of England's imperial system. To be sure, English authorities resisted this process. Following a theory called mercantilism, which viewed England and its colonies as a single economic unit controlled from London,

Parliament enacted a series of Navigation Acts from 1651 through 1733 to integrate the North American and West Indian trade into the larger imperial economy. In this view, the colonies would supply raw materials while importing manufactured products and consumer goods from England. In some ways mercantilism did stimulate colonial economic activity (encouraging shipbuilding, fisheries, tobacco cultivation, and the production of naval stores, for example). But in the economic as in the political realm, colonists increasingly looked to their own interests rather than those of distant England. Achieving independence, in short, was a process, not a single event.

Religion loomed large in colonial America, and ministers exerted intellectual and social leadership. Yet this was a diverse religious culture. No single denomination held sway throughout the colonies. Anglicans, numerous in Virginia, constituted a minority elsewhere. Puritan congregationalism was mostly confined to New England. Quakers, powerful in Pennsylvania, had little influence elsewhere. Even within each colony, enforcing religious conformity proved difficult. When Roger Williams, pastor of the Salem, Massachusetts, church, was banished in 1635 for his heterodox views, he and his followers simply migrated to nearby Rhode Island. In western Pennsylvania, Scots-Irish Presbyterians challenged the Quaker leadership in Philadelphia. In Virginia, Baptists and Methodists resisted the authority of the Church of England. By the late eighteenth century, Deists in Virginia and proto-Unitarians in New England rejected orthodox Christian dogma altogether. Some lamented this diversity, but in fact it stimulated religious vitality. In a free market of competing religious groups, with no established church, religion's overall influence thrived.

This diversity, coupled with the core Protestant belief in individual responsibility for one's own salvation, stimulated surges of religious enthusiasm that further undermined ecclesiastical hierarchies. A wave of revivalism in the 1740s, the so-called Great

Awakening, swept the colonies under the preaching of a touring English evangelist, George Whitefield, and a host of homegrown itinerants.

Jonathan Edwards of Massachusetts, an early proponent of the revival, terrified the unsaved with his sermon "Sinners in the Hands of an Angry God" (1741). A learned theologian as well as pastor and revivalist, Edwards drew upon current theories of the will in order to defend emotional preaching. While mastering the works of John Locke and other Enlightenment thinkers, Edwards reasserted orthodox Christian doctrine, including a Calvinist view of God's omnipotence and human sinfulness. His collected works extend to twenty-six volumes—an output cut short by his premature death in 1758 as he prepared to assume the presidency of Princeton College in New Jersey.

Preaching in welcoming churches or in the open air, revivalists called on sinners to repent; mere baptism or church membership would not suffice. Spawning missionary enterprises and new denominations, popular piety is another of the colonial era's enduring legacies. The means have changed—from open-air exhortation to televangelism and suburban megachurches—but evangelical faith and missionary zeal remain alive and well in twenty-first-century America.

The New England Puritans, with a strong sense of divine purpose, were confident of their special destiny. In a shipboard lecture en route to America, John Winthrop, Massachusetts' first governor, called the soon-to-be-founded settlement "a city on a hill," a model of God's ultimate plan for humanity. Elaborated by a succession of ministers, this sense of divine purpose arose from a particular reading of sacred history: God had chosen the Puritans to create in America a New Zion, as He had once chosen the Jews in ancient times. Sometimes reformulated in secular language, this deep-seated belief in America's unique role in history would long survive.

If the people proved unfaithful, however, these Puritan divines warned, retribution would follow—just as Jehovah had punished the Jews for their wickedness. Earthquakes, storms, Indian attacks, and even the 1692 witchcraft trials were interpreted as signs of God's displeasure. This guilt-ridden sense of decline from the higher standards of earlier times would also have a long afterlife in American religion and public life.

Although the contrast was sometimes overstated, colonial American society was characterized by less-rigid social hierarchies and gender roles than those generally found in Europe at the time. To be sure, even apart from slavery, colonial America was hardly the classless utopia some Enlightenment thinkers imagined. Every colony had its elite—ministers, lawyers, merchants; Virginia's great planters; New York's landed proprietors; Philadelphia's Quaker establishment; New England's shipmasters. Nine colleges founded in the colonial era, from Harvard in 1636 to Dartmouth in 1769, perpetuated these elites. And each colony had its middling ranks of independent farmers and urban craftsmen; and—lower still on the pecking order—day laborers, farm hands, and indentured servants.

Compared to much of Europe, however, the white population was less rigidly stratified, had higher literacy rates, and enjoyed greater opportunities for social mobility. The image of America as a more open, less hierarchical society, which would survive into an industrial age of great fortunes and grinding poverty, had its origin in partly mythic but also partly accurate memories of colonial society.

In terms of gender roles, the colonies replicated the patriarchal patterns of the era. Voting and public office were restricted to property-owning white males. Married women were barred from holding property or earning wages. A separation of spheres generally prevailed, with women performing domestic and child-rearing duties. In Boston in 1637, Anne Hutchinson was expelled from the church and banished from the colony for criticizing the minister's sermons at gatherings in her home. "You have stepped out of your place," one minister admonished her; "you [would] have rather been a husband than a wife, a preacher than a hearer."

Yet in actual practice, gender boundaries were not typically patrolled so rigidly, and women played respected social roles in their communities. Some pursued "male" occupations, particularly widows after the death of a male breadwinner. Further, in this pre-industrial age, women's "domestic" activities, from gardening and tending farm animals to baking, candle making, and sewing, were centrally important to their family's economic well-being. Some young women worked as domestic servants. Older women served the community as midwives or—particularly in New England—conducted "dame schools" in their homes for local children. In the gender realm, too, the relative openness of colonial life created opportunities for women to move beyond traditional roles, laying the groundwork for further changes in the nineteenth century and beyond.

A clash of empires: France versus England

Despite restive stirrings, the English colonists down to the 1760s had a compelling reason to welcome Britain's sheltering protection: a hostile French presence to the north and west. Following Jacques Cartier's explorations in the 1530s and the establishment of French fishing camps and trading posts along the St. Lawrence River, Samuel de Champlain founded Quebec in 1608. While French Catholic priests started missions, intrepid French fur traders, called *voyageurs* and *coureurs de bois* (wood runners), operated across present-day Michigan, Wisconsin, and Minnesota. Forts, missions, and trading posts from the St. Lawrence and the Great Lakes down the Mississippi to New Orleans (founded 1718) underscored France's imperial ambitions.

The English settlers viewed these developments with alarm. As early as 1654, Massachusetts militiamen drove the French from

Cape Breton Island. Over the next century, as France and England waged several wars, skirmishes between English colonists and French settlements persisted. In an unsuccessful 1755 raid on Fort Duquesne, a French outpost on the site of today's Pittsburgh, the twenty-three-year old George Washington served as aide-de-camp to British general Edward Braddock, who died in the fighting.

In the Seven Years' War (1756–63), France and Great Britain, with other European powers, battled for supremacy. The war's North American phase involved French and British troops, colonial militias, and each side's Indian allies. (Underscoring this latter aspect, the English colonists called the conflict the French and Indian War.) Fighting raged across the Ohio Valley, the Great Lakes, northern New York, and the heart of French power along the St. Lawrence. Twenty thousand colonial volunteers supplemented England's troops and naval forces. The British fared poorly at first, but under a vigorous new parliamentary leader, William Pitt, the tide turned. In 1759 an Anglo-American force defeated the French at Quebec. Montreal surrendered in 1760, ending the war's American phase. The Treaty of Paris (1763) confirmed England's imperial dominance in North America westward to the Mississippi River.

But this outcome only increased tensions in the restive American colonies. With the French threat removed, British rule seemed increasingly onerous. Relations worsened as the British government, by the Proclamation of 1763, restricted colonists' westward expansion, reserving the lands between the Appalachian Mountains and the Mississippi to the Indian inhabitants. Religious fears exacerbated the colonists' anger, since Britain granted full religious freedom to the thousands of French Catholics in its newly acquired territories. Further, Parliament sought to pay off its heavy war debt by increasing colonial taxes. The stage was set for a showdown.

Chapter 2

1763–1789: Revolution, Constitution, a new nation

Each day in Washington, DC, vacationing families and tourists from around the globe line up patiently at the National Archives to see the Declaration of Independence the Constitution. In respectful silence, visitors reverently filed past the vault-like display cases in the vast rotunda.

These faded parchments so solemnly enshrined today—"American Scriptures," in the words of one historian—date from a hectic era of imperial struggle, mob violence, bloody warfare, and political crisis. They reflect fierce debates, hard-headed compromises, and the intellectual creativity of statesmen who built the case for independence and then crafted a new nation's governing framework.

The path to independence

Saddled with debt from the Seven Years' War, ~~Parliament set~~ out to extract more revenue from the colonies. From London's perspective this seemed fair, since British troops had defeated the colonists' French foes. These postwar taxes and other measures angered many colonists, however, since the colonies lacked representation in Parliament.

In the Sugar Act (1764), the first of these measures, Parliament lowered duties on molasses the colonists imported from the

French West Indies but increased duties on other imported goods. To thwart smuggling, the act tightened inspection of colonial merchant ships and shifted smuggling cases from lenient local magistrates to Admiralty Courts headed by British judges.

Next came the Stamp Act (1765), requiring colonists to purchase special stamped paper for newspapers, diplomas, and legal documents, and even taxing dice and playing cards! While the Sugar Act served the dual purpose of raising revenue and regulating trade, the Stamp Act's sole aim was to increase taxes. As a further irritant, the 1765 Quartering Act required colonial taxpayers to house and feed British troops stationed in America.

British authorities pointed out that the colonists, while enjoying military protection and trading privileges, paid lower taxes than did Britons at home. But without representation, colonists protested, any tax violated their rights. In Virginia's House of Burgesses, Patrick Henry introduced resolutions denouncing the Act. Protests turned violent in Boston, where a mob hanged the tax collector in effigy and trashed the residence of Chief Justice Thomas Hutchinson, a Stamp Act defender. In October 1765, delegates from nine colonies met in New York City. Affirming colonial solidarity, this "Stamp Act Congress" passed resolutions denying Parliament's right to tax the colonies. Amid mounting protests, Parliament in 1766 repealed the Stamp Act but passed a "Declaratory Act" affirming its authority over the colonies.

Tensions eased with the Stamp Act's repeal and the advent of a new prime minister, William Pitt, who was popular in the colonies. But parliamentary leadership soon passed from the ailing Pitt to a hard-nosed Chancellor of the Exchequer, Charles Townshend. In a 1767 act dubbed the Townshend Duties, Parliament slapped duties on various products imported by the colonies and created a new revenue-collection bureaucracy, the American Board of Customs Commissioners. Attempting to appease colonists' sensitivities, Townshend differentiated these "external taxes" from "internal taxes" such as the Stamp Act. But in an influential 1767 pamphlet misleadingly titled *Letters from a Farmer in Pennsylvania*, the Philadelphia lawyer John Dickinson rejected this distinction.

As the dispute deepened, Boston's Samuel Adams distributed the Massachusetts Circular Letter to all the colonies denouncing Parliament's action. When several colonial legislatures endorsed Adams's letter, the royal governors dissolved them. The Sons of Liberty, a loose-knit organization originally formed to oppose the Stamp Act, revived, urging a boycott of British imports. In June 1768, a Boston mob attacked customs officials who had seized a ship (appropriately called *Liberty*) owned by merchant John Hancock. Partially relenting, Parliament repealed most of the Townshend Duties in 1770 but again asserted its authority by retaining the tax on tea the colonists imported. Ominously, London also ordered four thousand troops to Boston.

On March 5, 1770, British troops guarding the Boston customs house fired on stone-throwing protesters, killing five, including Crispus Attucks, an African American seaman. Outrage over the "Boston Massacre" quickly spread, fed by an inflammatory engraving of the incident by Boston silversmith Paul Revere.

In 1772, prodded by Samuel Adams, Massachusetts towns set up Committees of Correspondence to coordinate resistance and publicize colonial grievances "to the World." Other colonies followed suit. Ignoring the warning signals, Parliament in 1773 passed the Tea Act to help the struggling East India Company dispose of its surplus tea. While lowering (but not removing) the import duty, the act gave the East India Company monopolistic authority to sell its tea in America through special agents, undercutting local merchants.

Boston again became the flashpoint of opposition. On the night of December 16, 1773, after a tumultuous town meeting, some fifty men disguised as Indians boarded a British ship and dumped

342 chests of tea into the harbor. The "Boston Tea Party" outraged British authorities. Parliament passed a series of Coercive Acts (called the "Intolerable Acts" in America) closing Boston harbor and subjecting the colony to direct royal rule. Further alarming Protestant colonists, Parliament extended the boundaries of Catholic Quebec to include the trans-Appalachian west.

In September 1774, delegates from all thirteen colonies except Georgia gathered in Philadelphia. This first Continental Congress denounced the Coercive Acts, approved a boycott of British imports, and authorized military preparations. But the delegates also professed loyalty to George III and urged him to resist Parliament's oppressive measures.

Building a case for independence

As colonial politicians, pamphleteers, and preachers furiously produced pamphlets, newspaper essays, and sermons; some favored independence, others negotiation and compromise. Massachusetts's Thomas Hutchinson, now governor, argued that the economic and military benefits of being part of the British Empire surely outweighed "what are called English liberties." Most, however, denounced Parliament's taxes and regulatory measures. Tellingly, they drew their arguments from England's own history, especially the Glorious Revolution of 1689, which had repudiated the absolutist claims of James II and established a limited monarchy. Echoing some English radicals, they argued that the now-landed aristocrats in Parliament were conspiring with the Crown to trample individual rights. Just as Parliament had resisted the Crown in 1689, now Parliament must be resisted. They especially admired John Wilkes, a London journalist and member of Parliament who favored reforming that body to make it more representative.

Colonial pamphleteers also drew on English political writers, especially John Locke, who in *Two Treatises on Civil Government*

(1690) argued that all persons possess a natural right to life, liberty, and property; that governments exist to protect these rights; and that the consent of the governed represents the sole basis of political legitimacy. Setting a model for present-day America, colonial religious leaders plunged into the political fray. While some, especially Anglican priests, urged loyalty to Britain, others joined the denunciations. The Bible and the Protestant faith, they insisted, upheld the colonists' righteous cause. Some even identified George III and his ministers with the Antichrist, the demonic ruler foretold in Revelation.

At the popular level, protesters erected liberty poles on town squares and sang ballads supporting the colonists' cause. A poem in the *Boston Gazette* began:

> Come join in hand, brave Americans all
> And rouse your bold hearts at fair Liberty's call.

As protests mounted, war drew closer. Ignoring conciliatory proposals by William Pitt (now Lord Chatham) and Edmund Burke's eloquent speeches defending the colonists, Parliament on February 7, 1775, declared Massachusetts in rebellion. General Thomas Gage, commander of the British troops in Boston, was authorized to crush the uprising.

On April 19, seven hundred Redcoats marched from Boston toward nearby Concord, to seize a cache of hidden weapons. Racing ahead on horseback, Paul Revere and William Dawes warned of the British approach. In Lexington, armed townsmen confronted the troops. As shooting erupted, eight colonists died. Finding no weapons, the Redcoats returned to Boston under a hail of gunfire. By nightfall, the British had endured more than 270 casualties and the colonists nearly 100. On June 17, the Redcoats attacked armed colonists occupying Bunker Hill and Breeds Hill overlooking Boston. The colonists suffered more than 300 casualties, the British more than 1,000.

In Philadelphia, the Continental Congress sent a final appeal to George III, the so-called Olive Branch Petition, again expressing loyalty but urging a ceasefire in Boston, repeal of the Coercive Acts, and negotiations over disputed issues. King and Parliament rejected this gesture, aware that Congress had also authorized a Continental army under George Washington.

In revolutionary situations, a single event can sometimes trigger the final leap from hesitation to irrevocable action. Such a moment came in January 1776 when a recent British immigrant, Thomas Paine, published an incendiary pamphlet, *Common Sense*, eloquently calling for independence. "Everything that is right or reasonable pleads for separation," Paine declared. "The blood of the slain, the weeping voice of nature cries, 'tis time to part." Appealing to the American sense of destiny, he proclaimed: "The cause of America is in great measure the cause of all mankind. . . . We have it in our power to begin the world over." As for George III, Paine denounced the British monarch as the "royal brute." *Common Sense* spread like wildfire through the colonies, electrifying the Patriot cause.

The war for independence

"[T]hese United Colonies are, and of Right ought to be, *free and Independent States*." So proclaimed a declaration drafted in spring 1776 by a Continental Congress committee, with Thomas Jefferson, a Virginia planter and political leader, as principal author. It listed the "abuses and usurpations" by which George III had tried to impose an "absolute tyranny," denying the colonists' natural right to "life, liberty, and property." In the revision process, Congress changed "property" (John Locke's formulation) to the more resonant "pursuit of happiness." On July 4 Congress adopted the Declaration of Independence, now enshrined at the National Archives. In its first official act of diplomacy, Congress dispatched Benjamin Franklin as emissary to Paris. A respected Philadelphia politician, civic leader, and statesman, Franklin secured vital French loans and, ultimately, military support for the infant nation.

COMMON SENSE;

ADDRESSED TO THE

INHABITANTS

OF

AMERICA,

On the following interesting

SUBJECTS.

I. Of the Origin and Design of Government in general, with concise Remarks on the English Constitution.

II. Of Monarchy and Hereditary Succession.

III. Thoughts on the present State of American Affairs.

IV. Of the present Ability of America, with some miscellaneous Reflections.

Man knows no Master save creating HEAVEN,
Or those whom choice and common good ordain.

THOMSON.

PHILADELPHIA;
Printed, and Sold, by R. BELL, in Third-Street.

MDCCLXXVI.

2. Thomas Paine's incendiary pamphlet *Common Sense* (1776) swept the colonies, hastening the break with Great Britain and helping bring on the American Revolution.

The drive for independence divided Britain's American colonies. Canadians rejected Congress's plea to join the cause. The sugar planters in Britain's Caribbean colonies showed no interest. Even in the thirteen mainland colonies, around 20 percent of the white population, called Loyalists, opposed independence for economic, career, or personal reasons, including lingering attachment to England or fear of revolutionary chaos. Facing ostracism and even violence, many Loyalists fled to England or Canada.

As hostilities began, each side had strengths and weaknesses. The British possessed a powerful navy and a disciplined army, both commanded by seasoned officers and buttressed by hired German mercenaries. But despite some Loyalist support, the British were fighting in enemy territory, with dangerously long supply lines, under conditions unsuited to conventional military tactics or set-piece battles.

The Continental army relied on poorly paid citizen-soldiers prone to drift away when their enlistment ended or farm duties called. But the colonists had crucial advantages. They were fighting on their home turf, and in George Washington they had a commander whose tactical skills steadily improved. Above all, Britain's European rivals, France, Spain, and the Netherlands, provided critical strategic support. Foreign volunteers were important as well. The twenty-year-old Marquis de Lafayette, arriving from France, joined Washington as aide-de-camp. The Prussian general Friedrich von Steuben played a vital role in training Washington's undisciplined soldiers and preparing a standard manual of arms and maneuvers.

After the Concord and Bunker Hill debacles, the British left Boston and, under General William Howe, shifted to Long Island, intent on driving a wedge between Virginia and Massachusetts. A naval fleet under Admiral Richard Howe (William's brother) hovered off shore. Besting Washington's army in several skirmishes, Howe in September 1776 occupied New York City, a Loyalist stronghold.

Retreating across New Jersey, Washington's army crossed the Delaware River into Pennsylvania. Successful counterattacks on British garrisons in New Jersey boosted Patriot morale, but in September 1777 Howe defeated the Continental army at Brandywine Creek and occupied Philadelphia. As Congress retreated, Washington's ragged troops spent a miserable winter at nearby Valley Forge. "These are times that try men's souls," wrote Thomas Paine in a new pamphlet, *The Crisis*.

Meanwhile, British troops under General John Burgoyne marched from Quebec southward along Lake Champlain and the Hudson River, hoping to join Howe, moving up the Hudson from New York, and a British-Iroquois force advancing from the west, cutting off New England. But Burgoyne's invasion faltered under attack by local militias and a Patriot army commanded by General Horatio Gates. On October 17, 1777, at Saratoga, New York, Burgoyne surrendered. With this defeat, the French (already secretly providing funds) recognized American independence and pledged direct military aid. The Netherlands and Spain backed the American cause as well.

Abandoning their northern strategy, the British looked southward. In 1778–79 they gained control of Georgia, and in May 1780 captured Charleston. At the Battle of Camden, South Carolina (August 1780), General George Cornwallis's army defeated an American force. But Patriot troops under General Nathanael Greene turned the tide in brutal fighting in the Carolina backcountry that included torture and civilian massacres.

In spring 1781, Cornwallis marched his weakened army to Virginia's Yorktown peninsula to await reinforcements and supplies. Here they were trapped by Washington's Continental army, redeploycd from Pennsylvania. A French fleet brought fresh troops and blocked a British escape by sea. On October 19, 1781, as a military band played "A World Turned Upside Down," Cornwallis surrendered.

The peace commission, meeting the British negotiators in Paris, included an odd couple, dour, moralistic John Adams of Massachusetts and the worldly Benjamin Franklin. But negotiations went forward, and in the Treaty of Paris (1783), the British recognized American independence.

The peoples of America in a revolutionary age

Though excluded from formal political participation, many American women supported the Patriot cause by boycotting British imports, including tea. (The national preference for coffee dates from this era.) Substituting homespun for British textiles signaled one's resistance to Parliamentary taxation.

During the war, women gained managerial experience running farms and businesses for absent husbands and fathers. Elite women of Philadelphia, styling themselves Daughters of Liberty, raised funds for the Continental army. Some women found gender implications in revolutionary ideology. If the framers of the new government failed to "remember the Ladies," John Adams's wife, Abigail, warned him in 1776, only half in jest, "we . . . will not hold ourselves bound by any Laws in which we have no voice, or Representation."

Native Americans maneuvered precariously amid the imperial struggles. In 1763, Indians along the Great Lakes attacked British forts in an uprising known as Pontiac's Rebellion. The Proclamation of 1763 promised to respect Indian rights, but clashes continued as settlers pushed westward. During the Revolutionary War, economic ties, land conflicts, and other considerations influenced each tribe's loyalties and alliances. In the North Carolina backcountry, the Cherokee allied with the British and attacked colonialists' encroaching settlements. In the Northwest Territory, local militia under a young Virginian, George Rogers Clark, brutally attacked Shawnee, Delaware, Wyandot, and Mingo settlements. In upstate New York, pro-British Iroquois battled Continental troops allied with Tuscarora and Oneida warriors. Overall, England's defeat hastened white settlers' expansion into Indian lands. "Victory" for the colonists had very different meaning for Native Americans.

For the colonies' more than half-million African Americans, most of them enslaved, the imperial conflict brought opportunities and hazards. When a London court in 1772 freed James Somersett, a Massachusetts slave whose master had brought him to England, other American slaves looked to England as a beacon of freedom. In 1775 when Lord Dunmore, Virginia's royal governor, offered freedom to all able-bodied male slaves who would support the British, about a thousand responded. Eventually some 20,000 southern slaves flocked to the British side. Only a few gained freedom, however; most succumbed to illness or were recaptured.

In the North, by contrast, many slaves and free blacks embraced the Patriot cause. Some even joined local militias or the Continental army. George Washington (himself a slave owner) rejected proposals to free slaves who served in the military, laconically warning that this would "render slavery more irksome for those still in it." Nevertheless, talk of natural rights highlighted the paradox of slavery and stirred antislavery sentiments across the North. As a Rhode Island slave who escaped from his master later recalled: "[W]hen I saw liberty poles and people all engaged for the support of freedom, I could not but . . . be pleased." Abolition lay decades in the future, but the American Revolution laid the groundwork.

Creating a nation

Having proclaimed their independence, Americans confronted the challenge of self-government. In 1777, with the war still raging, Congress adopted the Articles of Confederation. Under this framework, Congress recorded some notable achievements, including the Treaty of Paris, securing American independence, and the Northwest Ordinance (1787), providing for the surveying, settlement, and formation of states in the territory bounded by the Appalachians, the Great Lakes, and the Mississippi and Ohio Rivers. One notable provision funded public education through land sales. The ordinance prohibited slavery in the region and pledged to honor Indian treaties—the latter provision soon violated.

Despite these achievements, the confederation proved weak. With no executive or judicial branches, it had only a unicameral Congress, elected annually, with one vote per state, whatever its population. Congress could issue currency, deliver mail, and negotiate treaties but could not impose taxes, regulate trade, or raise an army. With memories of parliamentary excesses still raw, the Articles of Confederation deliberately created a feeble central government, preserving full sovereignty to the states. A postwar depression highlighted these weaknesses. Social unrest and demands for debt relief, culminating in Shays's Rebellion, a 1786 uprising by Massachusetts farmers, alarmed conservatives and the wealthy, increasing pressures for a stronger central government.

In February 1787, Congress invited the states to send delegates to Philadelphia to revise the articles. All responded except Rhode Island, fearful of losing the power to impose import duties. Convening in May, the delegates abandoned the articles entirely and set about crafting a new Constitution. Through the hot summer they debated, defending their states' interests, trading political and social views, and drawing upon the colonies' long experience of self-government. They resolved differences between large and small states by creating a bicameral Congress: a Senate with two senators from each state, and a House of Representatives with each state's delegation determined by its population.

The debates, recorded by Virginia's James Madison, revealed the delegates' knowledge of political theory and of actual governments from antiquity to the present. Many cited Lockean natural-rights theory (also identified with the Scottish philosopher David Hume), upholding popular consent as the source of governmental legitimacy. They also invoked republican theorists, including the statesman Niccolò Machiavelli of Renaissance Florence, who saw civic virtue and concern for the public good as anchors of stability. Influenced by Thomas Hobbes's *Leviathan* (1651) and Calvinist theology, conservative delegates stressed the need for a strong government to prevent social chaos and civil war—what Hobbes called "the war of all against all." *The Spirit of the Laws* (1748) by the French theorist Baron de Montesquieu, arguing for the separation of powers as a safeguard against despotism, also proved influential.

The document that emerged reflected the delegates' fear of tyranny—the danger they had just fought a war to resist. Dividing power between the federal government and the states, it also carefully parceled out the federal government's own powers among three branches: the bicameral legislature; an executive branch headed by a president; and a judiciary with a Supreme Court chosen by presidential nomination with Senate approval. Counterbalancing restraints limited each branch's power. The president could veto a congressional bill, for example, but Congress could overturn a veto by a two-thirds vote. In an age of monarchies and hereditary aristocracies, the Constitution, beginning "We the people of the United States," established a republic, answerable to the people through elections. But it also revealed the delegates' suspicions of "democracy"—a term generally associated with mob rule. Senators would be elected by state legislatures, not by popular vote. Citizens would not vote for presidents or vice presidents directly, but for "electors" who would make that decision. Only male property owners would vote in federal elections. (The Constitution granted federal voting rights to everyone qualified to vote for the lower house of their state legislature. At this time, every state imposed property requirements for voting.) At slaveholders' insistence, slavery was embedded into the nation's founding charter. (Embarrassed about

27

mentioning slavery in a document establishing a republic, the delegates referred euphemistically to "all other Persons" [Art. I, Sec. 2] and "Persons held to service or labor" [Art. IV, Sec. 2].) The Constitution required that slaves escaping from one state to another be returned to their masters; counted three-fifths of the slave population in apportioning representation in the House of Representatives; and even permitted the slave trade to continue for twenty years.

In September, when Congress submitted the Constitution to the state legislatures for ratification, suspicions ran high. Small farmers feared urban commercial and banking interests. Vocal opponents, including Virginia's Patrick Henry, charged that the Constitution failed to safeguard individual or states' rights, raising the specter of despotism. But the Constitution's supporters, known as Federalists, included the most prominent Revolutionary leaders. Addressing the opponents' fears, they pledged to support a Bill of Rights, which in fact was added to the Constitution in 1791 in the form of ten amendments, including one reserving to the states or to the people all powers not specifically granted to the federal government.

The most notable contribution to the ratification debate, and to the vast literature of political theory, was *The Federalist*— eighty-five essays published in New York City newspapers under the pseudonym "Publius" and written mostly by Alexander Hamilton and James Madison, with a few by John Jay. While Hamilton made the case for a strong federal government, Madison explained the Constitution's checks and balances. Addressing fears that a republican government could not succeed in a large nation, Madison in "Federalist 10" argued just the reverse. America's diverse economic, geographic, and other interests would counterbalance each other, he contended, assuring overall stability.

Opinion gradually turned favorable, and by summer 1788 the required nine states had ratified, including Massachusetts, Virginia, and even doubtful New York. In the first federal elections that November, George Washington emerged as the unanimous choice for president. On April 30 in New York City, wearing a plain brown suit rather than his military uniform, Washington took the oath of office. Various honorific titles were proposed, but Washington made his preference clear: "Mr. President."

In a remarkable thirteen years, thirteen British colonies had won independence and established a new nation. The 1787 Constitution, though a document of its time, and stained by references to slavery, stands as a remarkable achievement, creating the first modern republican government. In coming centuries it would prove adaptable to changed circumstances, yet faithful to the founders' vision.

How would the United States fare as it addressed urgent domestic problems and made its debut on the world stage? That remained to be seen.

Chapter 3
1789–1850: The promise and perils of nationhood

As the new government took shape, political parties emerged at home and American diplomats maneuvered in a dangerous world. These formative decades also brought social and economic changes, reformist enthusiasms and religious ferment, and a surge of cultural creativity that some have grandly labeled the American Renaissance. One historian summed it all up in a phrase: "Freedom's ferment."

The rise of party politics

When George Washington died in 1799, after having served two presidential terms, he was already firmly enshrined in the American pantheon, eulogized by fellow Virginian Henry Lee as "First in war, first in peace, first in the hearts of his countrymen." But mourning for the hero of the Revolution could not conceal the political divisions roiling the new nation. The Constitution does not mention political parties; indeed, the founders abhorred the very idea. Washington's 1796 Farewell Address to the American people denounced "factions" promoted by "artful and enterprising" politicians.

Yet two members of Washington's own cabinet, Treasury Secretary Alexander Hamilton and Secretary of State Thomas Jefferson, personified the differing interests and ideologies fueling party conflict. Hamilton, an immigrant from the British West Indies, had served on Washington's staff during the war. Fearful of democracy, he advocated a strong government allied with propertied interests. To stimulate economic development and link the government to the commercial class he created the Bank of the United States (1791) and pushed legislation by which the government redeemed at face value the depreciated wartime currency issued by Congress, now mostly held by speculators. Hamilton also proposed that the federal government pay off the states' war debts. Since this mainly benefitted the northern states, Hamilton, Jefferson, and Madison brokered a compromise under which the national capital would be in the South, on land ceded by Virginia and Maryland—today's Washington, DC. During the 1794 Whiskey Rebellion, when farmers of western Pennsylvania resisted a federal tax on distilled spirits, Hamilton donned his uniform and, with Washington, personally led troops to quash the protests. Hamilton's supporters comprised the nation's first political party, the Federalists. Under his leadership (until his fatal 1804 duel with Aaron Burr), the party, centered in the North, attracted creditors, merchants, entrepreneurs, and wealthy landowners.

Jefferson represented different interests and a different worldview. Suspicious of big government and big cities, he idealized virtuous tillers of the soil. Though a slaveholder, he embraced the natural-rights philosophy of John Locke and more radical theorists. The Democratic-Republican Party that rallied around Jefferson attracted small farmers, urban workers, and states'-rights advocates suspicious of Hamilton's activist program. Partisan newspaper editors egged on the division.

When the French Revolution began in 1789, Jefferson initially welcomed it. The United States with its own revolutionary history, he reasoned, should embrace such movements elsewhere. The Federalists, by contrast, were appalled, particularly as French aristocrats and even the nation's monarchs went to the guillotine. When England declared war on France in 1793, Federalists welcomed the action. As Hamilton's influence grew, Jefferson left the administration in 1793.

Pursuing the war with France, British warships captured U.S. vessels trading with the French West Indies and seized crewmembers suspected of desertion from the Royal Navy. London addressed some U.S. grievances in a 1795 treaty negotiated by the Federalist John Jay, but Democratic-Republicans denounced Jay's failure to insist more vigorously on America's neutral rights.

Jefferson was elected vice president in 1796 but in an administration headed by Federalist John Adams. In 1798 congressional Federalists passed the Alien and Sedition Acts, a panicky response to events in France. Under these laws, Federalist judges and juries targeted not only suspect aliens but also Jeffersonian newspaper editors. In 1800 Jefferson won the presidency, marking a peaceful transfer of power from one party to another, an encouraging sign for future governmental stability. His administration began auspiciously with the Louisiana Purchase, but his second-term efforts to protect U.S. shipping proved contentious. With England and France (now ruled by Napoleon Bonaparte) again at war, each side tried to prevent U.S. trade with the other. Jefferson's response, an embargo on exports to force the warring powers to recognize U.S. neutral rights, accomplished little and was widely denounced for its negative economic impact, especially by northern merchants and shippers, already hostile to Jefferson and his party.

In 1812, under Jefferson's successor James Madison, Britain's continued harassment of U.S. shipping erupted into war. An attempted U.S. invasion of Canada, demanded by congressional "War Hawks," led to some naval victories on Lake Erie but otherwise failed. Worse still, in August 1814 British forces captured Washington, DC, and burned the new presidential mansion. (First Lady Dolley Madison saved Gilbert Stuart's portrait of George Washington as she fled to safety.)

With "Mr. Madison's War" deeply unpopular in New England, some Federalist politicians contemplated secession. But in December 1814, as Britain faced reverses in Europe, negotiators meeting in Ghent, Belgium, signed a treaty ending the war. The news failed to reach British commanders besieging New Orleans, however, and on January 8, 1815, the U.S. militia under General Andrew Jackson killed 291 attacking Redcoats, including their commandeer, and wounded nearly 1,300.

The Ghent Treaty left most U.S. grievances unresolved, but the United States had at least avoided defeat in this "Second War of Independence," and the New Orleans slaughter unleashed a burst of nationalistic pride. Federalist opposition faded, and Madison won a second term. In 1823, suspecting French meddling in Cuba, a Spanish colony, London proposed a joint British-U.S. warning against such intervention. However, Secretary of State John Quincy Adams cautioned President James Monroe (Madison's successor, elected in 1816) that America must not appear as a mere "cockboat in the wake of the British man of war." Instead, Monroe released a statement, drafted by Adams, warning European powers against colonial ventures in the Western Hemisphere. The so-called Monroe Doctrine underscored America's growing confidence in world affairs.

In 1824 Andrew Jackson received the most votes for president, but not an Electoral College majority. This threw the contest into the House of Representatives, where Henry Clay of Kentucky, another contender, supported John Quincy Adams, the second-place winner. Upon taking office, Adams appointed Clay secretary of state, leading outraged Jackson supporters to denounce the "corrupt bargain." Adams proposed a visionary program of national planning, including federal support for agriculture, commerce, and transportation, as well as a national observatory and national university. States'-rights advocates professed dismay at Adams's vision, the "corrupt bargain" accusations persisted, and Adams lost his second-term bid.

Despite the Federalist Party's demise, Chief Justice John Marshall perpetuated its strong-government, pro-business principles. Nominated to the Supreme Court by John Adams in 1801, Marshall served until his death in 1835. In a series of landmark cases, Marshall affirmed the primacy of federal over state law, and the judiciary's power to determine the constitutionality of laws passed by Congress. In *Dartmouth College v. Woodward* (1819), Marshall upheld the inviolability of contract, a principle crucial to capitalist enterprise. Further asserting federal power, the Marshall court in *McCullough v. Maryland* (1819) ruled unconstitutional a Maryland tax on the Second Bank of the United States, incorporated by Congress in 1816.

A political watershed came in 1828 with Andrew Jackson's election as president. Jackson differed radically from the elite figures who had hitherto governed the nation. Born in South Carolina, orphaned at fourteen, Jackson migrated to Tennessee and built a self-made career as a politician, planter, and militia officer. Winning fame at the 1815 Battle of New Orleans, he embodied the individualistic, egalitarian spirit of the West. Jubilant supporters poured into Washington for their hero's inauguration. Jackson won a second term in 1832, defeating another westerner, Henry Clay, of the conservative Whig Party.

Jackson's victory reflected broader demographic and political changes. Surging migration to the interior plus the end of property requirements for voting had broadened the electorate to include southern cotton planters; western farmers and entrepreneurs; and eastern laborers and factory workers. These voters rallied to Jackson, and by 1832 the movement had a name: the Democratic Party. Jackson's close-knit inner circle, dubbed his "Kitchen Cabinet," including newspaper editors Amos Kendall and Francis Preston Blair, played a key role.

Suspicious of elites and entrenched interests, Jacksonians opposed high tariffs protecting domestic manufacturers. They also disliked the Second Bank of the United States (BUS), a federally chartered, Philadelphia-based institution with branches in eight states. To Jackson, the BUS embodied the "money power"—a colossus stifling the expansive energies of the interior, including four hundred freewheeling state banks. Viewing his battle with the "Monster Bank" as a personal struggle with its head, Nicholas Biddle, Jackson vetoed Congress's early renewal of the bank's charter in 1832 and then fatally weakened it by withdrawing federal funds. The so-called Bank War helped bring on a business panic in 1837 and several years of hard times, but for Jackson it represented a victory of "the people" over entrenched interests. In retrospect, it seems primarily a confrontation between established elites and emerging entrepreneurial and commercial forces in the burgeoning west and urban centers.

Although suspicious of federal power, Jackson vigorously resisted when Vice President John C. Calhoun, a political rival, led a movement in Calhoun's home state, South Carolina, to "nullify" the 1832 Tariff, which southerners considered oppressive. When Jackson threatened force, the nullifiers backed off.

While conservative elites deplored the raw crudity of Jacksonian democracy, it did express the dynamism of an ambitious, expansive white population. In 1840, copying the Democrats' innovative campaign tactics, the conservative, business-oriented Whigs mobilized torchlight parades, miniature log cabins, and hard cider to send Ohio's William Henry Harrison, an aging politician and veteran of the Indian wars, to the White House. Unfortunately, Harrison contracted pneumonia after delivering an interminable open-air inaugural address and died a month later.

A dynamic society

Secure in their independence, Americans exuded confidence (some called it bumptious arrogance) as the century advanced. Expansive Fourth of July orators found many reasons to justify the upbeat mood. By 1850 the U.S. white population, fueled by immigration and high fertility, exceeded twenty-one million, a fivefold increase since 1790. In one decade alone, 1845–54, nearly three million newcomers arrived, including desperate Irish escaping a devastating potato blight. While many immigrants pushed on westward, others settled in coastal cities, finding employment as manual laborers, domestic servants, and factory workers.

The nation grew geographically as well. In 1803, to fund his European wars, Napoleon offered to sell Louisiana for $15 million, and U.S. diplomats in Paris quickly accepted. This vast territory, some 830,000 square miles, unfolded westward from the Mississippi to the Rocky Mountains. President Jefferson, overcoming Federalist protests and his own constitutional scruples, approved the purchase and authorized the Lewis and Clark Expedition (1804–6) to explore the new territory. Spain ceded Florida to the United States in 1819, and in 1846 the United States, by agreement with Great Britain, acquired present-day Washington, Oregon, and Idaho.

In 1836 Anglo-American settlers in Texas, a part of Spanish Mexico, declared independence. Mexican troops killed 186 independence fighters defending San Antonio's Alamo mission, but Texans led by Sam Houston, inspired by the battle cry "Remember the Alamo," defeated Mexican forces at the Battle of San Jacinto soon after, securing Texas independence. In 1845 Texans voted for statehood.

As Mexico and the United States disputed their border, expansionists proclaimed America's "Manifest Destiny" to push ever westward. In May 1846, after a disputed border clash, President James Polk, a Tennessee Democrat, secured a congressional declaration of war against Mexico. After several U.S. victories, General Winfield Scott occupied Mexico City in September. As Mexico capitulated, the United States acquired some half-million square miles, including the present states of

Arizona, California, Nevada, and Utah. California, its population swollen by an 1848 gold rush, entered the union in 1850. Within a single lifetime, a nation of thirteen states along the Atlantic coast had become a continental power, stretching from ocean to ocean.

As settlers poured westward, new states entered the Union, beginning with Ohio in 1803. The newcomers traveled by turnpike, canal, and rail. The National Road, America's first interstate highway, authorized by Congress in 1806, began in Maryland and reached Vandalia, Illinois, by 1839. The Erie Canal, linking the Hudson River and Lake Erie, opened in 1825. As canal projects by states and local entrepreneurs proliferated, railroads soon joined the grid. Charles Carroll, a signer of the Declaration of Independence, laid the cornerstone for the Baltimore and Ohio railroad on July 4, 1828. By 1850 America boasted nine thousand miles of track.

Population growth, geographic expansion, and a growing transportation infrastructure fueled economic development. Agriculture—cotton and tobacco in the South, grains and livestock in the North and West—remained central. The annual value of America's (mostly agricultural) exports reached $250 million by the 1850s. But industry grew as well, facilitated by skilled immigrants with knowledge of British production technologies. In 1822 Boston investors opened a mechanized cotton mill along the Merrimack River in nearby Lowell. Young farm women comprised the initial workforce, but immigrants soon replaced them.

Soon, factories across the North were manufacturing textiles, shoes, clocks, guns, machinery, railroad cars, and myriad other products. As steam engines replaced mill wheels, the annual value of U.S. factory production neared $2 billion by 1860. The great era of industrialization lay ahead, but a solid foundation already existed by mid-century.

Social conflict, reformist ferment

Amid boasts of national progress, darker realities intruded. With factory wages at subsistence levels, urban poverty increased and class divisions widened. Irish Catholic immigrants faced hostility and sometimes violence. The anti-immigrant American Party, founded in 1843, won broad support.

Westward expansion devastated native peoples. In an 1811 battle in Indiana Territory, U.S. troops under William Henry Harrison defeated an Indian confederacy loyal to the Shawnee leader Tecumseh. No longer able to play off one European power against another, Indians in the Northwest Territory were pushed steadily westward or squeezed onto reservations. An 1832 attempt by Sauk and other Indian tribes under Chief Black Hawk to reclaim ancestral lands east of the Mississippi was brutally repulsed.

In the South, the Indian Removal Act (1830) authorized the expulsion of the Cherokee and other tribes from their ancestral lands. Chief Justice Marshall upheld the tribes' claims in two important cases, but state officials and President Jackson defied him. "Mr. Marshall has made his decision," Jackson sneered; "Now let him enforce it." When "a few savage hunters" had been expelled, said Jackson in his 1830 State of the Union address, the South would "advance rapidly in population, wealth and power." Once praised as the personification of "the rise of American democracy" and "the era of the common man," Jackson is now seen in a less celebratory light. Thousands died as Indian families, forcibly uprooted by U.S. troops, trekked to present-day Oklahoma along a route later called the Trail of Tears.

Unsettling social changes created fertile soil for religious revivals, utopian ventures, and reform movements. While periodic revivals blazed across the southern frontier, Charles Finney's revivals, starting in 1825, attracted throngs in northern cities. Many New Englanders responded to William Miller's prediction of

Jesus's return in 1844. Others followed Joseph Smith, who in 1830 published the *Book of Mormon*, which he claimed to have discovered and translated with supernatural assistance. Echoing the New England Puritans' sense of destiny, this work portrayed North America as singled out for special divine purposes.

As cities and factories burgeoned, the 1840s saw the founding of celibate communities from Maine to Kentucky by the United Society of Believers in Christ's Second Appearing, or Shakers, an English sect whose followers came to America in 1774. These communities attracted notice for their unique worship practices; skilled craftsmanship; and marketing of seeds and other useful products. Other communes, religious and secular, sprang up in Iowa, Pennsylvania, New Harmony, Indiana, and Brook Farm near Boston. Some followed principles propounded by a French visionary, Charles Fourier. Perhaps naively, the founders hoped that cooperation, rather than competitive individualism, would spread to the larger society.

Jesus did not return in 1844; Joseph Smith was murdered in 1844 (though his new religion lived on); and the utopian communities gradually faded. But longings for a transformed society persisted, and reform movements proliferated. Temperance advocates preached sobriety; Sabbatarians urged Sunday closing laws; and others advocated more humane treatment of prisoners and the insane. Horace Mann of Massachusetts campaigned for better public schools. The antislavery cause won adherents—while stirring opposition—across the North.

With the rise of an urban middle class, some women questioned traditional gender roles and patriarchal assumptions. In 1848 Elizabeth Cady Stanton of Seneca Falls, New York, the Philadelphia Quaker Lucretia Mott, and others announced a Woman's Rights Convention in Seneca Falls. Its manifesto, echoing the Declaration of Independence, proclaimed "all men *and women* are created equal" and demanded full gender equality. Many hurdles lay

3. Reflecting an age of moral reform, this 1851 temperance banner depicts a young man rejecting a proffered glass of liquor from a dark-gowned temptress in favor of a glass of pure water offered by a white-clad young maiden.

ahead, but the women's movement had been launched. (One young attendee at the 1848 convention lived to cast her first vote in 1920.)

These religious movements and reform campaigns reflected a desire to recover the revolutionary-era vision of a transformed society. Amid social changes and problems, some still dreamed of the "new world" Thomas Paine had evoked in the heady days of 1776.

Art and culture in a new nation

"Who reads an American book . . . or looks at an American picture or statue?" sneered a Scottish journalist in 1820. Stung by such charges, artists and writers strove to add a cultural dimension to the nation's political and economic achievements. In the early post-revolutionary era, painters Gilbert Stuart, John Trumbull, and others memorialized the Founders and heroic scenes from the Revolutionary War and the Constitutional Convention. By the 1830s, influenced by the European Romantic movement's discovery of wilderness sublimity, picturesque villages, and ancient ruins, American artists sought inspiration in nature. Amid encroaching factories, cities, and railroads, Asher Durand and others painted romantic vistas of the Hudson and Connecticut Rivers, the Catskill and Adirondack Mountains, and the awe-inspiring Niagara Falls.

Striking an apprehensive note, Thomas Cole traced a society's progression from unspoiled innocence to cataclysmic destruction in a series of four allegorical paintings, *The Course of Empire* (1833–36). George Inness's *The Lackawanna Valley* (1855), commissioned by a railroad company, included a minuscule train and roundhouse in an otherwise bucolic Pennsylvania landscape.

Writers, too, probed the evolving national experience. In his short story "Rip Van Winkle" (1820), Washington Irving romanticized colonial days while acknowledging inevitable change. James Fenimore Cooper in *The Last of the Mohicans* (1826) and other novels romantically evoked the fate of Indians and woodsmen as farms and towns steadily advanced. Edgar Allan Poe offered a darker version of Romanticism with creepy tales such as "The Fall of the House of Usher." But Poe, too, acknowledged contemporary realities in stories like "The Man of the Crowd" (1840) and "The Mystery of Marie Rogêt" (1842), set in Paris but based on an actual murder in New York City.

The 1850s brought a burst of literary creativity. In *The Scarlet Letter* (1850) and *The House of the Seven Gables* (1851), Nathaniel Hawthorne explored his New England ancestors' sin-obsessed world. Herman Melville's *Moby-Dick* (1851) drew on his experiences at sea to document life aboard a whaling vessel while probing the crewmembers' emotional lives and tracing the captain's obsessive and increasingly metaphorical pursuit of a great white whale. Neglected at the time, *Moby-Dick* today ranks among the classics of American literature. In *Leaves of Grass* (1855), the Brooklyn journalist-turned-poet Walt Whitman evoked the sprawling diversity of American life while acknowledging his homosexuality with a candor that contemporaries found unsettling.

Meanwhile, a group of New England "Transcendentalists," influenced by the German idealist philosopher Immanuel Kant and British poets and writers like Samuel Taylor Coleridge, William Wordsworth, and Thomas Carlyle, sought to transcend mundane experience to the realm of pure perception. Their leader, Ralph Waldo Emerson of Concord, Massachusetts, left the Unitarian ministry in 1832 to write and lecture. In an 1832 Harvard Divinity School address and in *Nature* (1836), Emerson rejected religious dogma in favor of a more intuitive quest for truth.

Yet while valuing individual insight, the Transcendentalists also sought to elevate culture and society. The Brook Farm utopian community in Massachusetts was a Transcendentalist project. In "The American Scholar" (1837), Emerson deplored Americans' slavish intellectual deference to Europe and called for a confident national culture rooted in American experience. One contemporary called it America's "intellectual declaration of independence." In *Woman in the Nineteenth Century* (1845), Margaret Fuller, editor of the Transcendentalist magazine *The Dial*, argued that a feminist component was essential to the cultural awakening Emerson envisioned.

Emerson's Concord neighbor Henry Thoreau was an early proponent of ecological awareness, keen observer of nature and society, and intermittent political activist. Thoreau was briefly jailed in 1846 for refusing to pay his taxes, in protest against the Mexican War and the southern slave owners who supported it. His *Civil Disobedience* (1849), defending passive resistance to unjust laws, has inspired generations of reformers and activists. In *Walden* (1854), a record of his two years living in a cabin on Walden Pond, Thoreau reflected on contemporary life in a nation experiencing rapid social and technological changes.

Along with high-minded writers and intellectuals, antebellum America spawned a raucous popular culture, anticipating today's reality TV and supermarket tabloids. In New York City, amid brothels, taverns, and beer gardens, penny newspapers like James Gordon Bennett's *New York Herald* offered sensational accounts of urban life. Music halls featured Stephen Foster's sentimental ballads and crude parodies of blacks and immigrants. The 1836 murder of Helen Jewett, a beautiful prostitute, was one of many scandalous events that elicited both salacious journalistic accounts and alarmed attention by moral reformers. This, too, was part of life in the young republic.

America through others' eyes

Foreign visitors offered observations on American life in these formative years. The intrepid Englishwoman Frances Trollope arrived with her children in 1827 after her husband's financial reverses. Briefly visiting a Tennessee utopian community, she spent two years as a shopkeeper in Cincinnati. Her bestselling *Domestic Manners of the Americans* (1832) offered shrewd if jaundiced observations on Americans' prudery, boastfulness, coarse manners, sharp practices, and emotional religious revivals.

The Frenchman Alexis de Tocqueville, who arrived in 1831 to study the U.S. prison system, probed more deeply in his two-volume *Democracy in America* (1835, 1840). Tocqueville saw the United States as the prototype of an emerging egalitarian democratic order, lacking an aristocracy and governed by majority rule. In his view, this new order encouraged individualism (a word he coined) while maintaining order through the influence of religion, public opinion, and voluntary associations—enduring features of American life still today.

Underlying the creativity and ferment of antebellum America lay the inescapable reality of slavery—a reality that mocked the national ideology of freedom and equality. Conflicts over slavery, Tocqueville reflected, could lead to "the most horrific of civil wars." Thirty years after his visit, these fears would tragically be realized.

Chapter 4
1850–1865: Slavery and Civil War

In August 1619, a Dutch trading vessel sold twenty Africans as indentured servants in Jamestown, Virginia. Thus began a process that would shape American history. By 1860, 4.4 million African Americans lived in the United States, nearly 90 percent of them slaves.

The story has many dimensions. Slavery undergirded the southern economy and roiled national politics. Slaves who resisted; slaves who sustained a vibrant culture against heavy odds; white Americans who confronted the contradiction between slavery and their professed political and religious principles—all comprise part of the story. The Civil War ended slavery, but the struggle for full equality—the promise of the Declaration of Independence—would take far longer.

Slavery in antebellum America

Throughout the colonial era, slavery existed in all of England's North American colonies and the Caribbean. Indeed, the 4.8 million enslaved Africans brought to the British West Indies vastly exceeded the 360,000 delivered to the mainland colonies. Sugarcane production dominated the British (and French) Caribbean island colonies to meet Europe's growing taste for sugar. Slavemasters were harsh, disease and malnutrition rampant, and the mortality rate extremely high.

The northern states gradually abolished slavery after independence, leaving it confined to the South. Even there, with soil depletion and emancipation movements, its days seemed numbered. But British and New England textile mills demanded cotton, and Eli Whitney's cotton gin (1793), which mechanized the removal of seeds from the bolls, increased the crop's profitability. Rice, tobacco, and sugarcane remained important, but by 1830 "King Cotton" ruled, with plantations stretching from South Carolina to Texas. In 1860 cotton accounted for nearly 60 percent of U.S. exports by value.

As cotton plantations spread, so did slavery. Only a minority of southern whites owned slaves, but with some twenty-three hundred planters holding more than a hundred slaves, the region's prosperity depended on enslaved workers. Even the Chesapeake region participated in the cotton economy, as tobacco planters sold "surplus" slaves to cotton planters in the interior. While commerce, factories, and free-labor agriculture transformed the North's economy, the South followed a different course—one fatefully entangled with slavery.

African American life under slavery

The system denied enslaved persons' basic humanity and made a mockery of natural-rights theory. Slave owners generally denied slaves even a rudimentary education, fearing it would foment unrest. While some slaves worked as household servants, most were field hands. Owners, viewing slaves as a labor source and trading commodity, encouraged reproduction with little regard for marriage bonds or family ties. Plantation owners' free access to female slaves resulted in widespread mixed-race births. Under state slave codes, the offspring of such relationships were slaves. Some masters were brutal, others milder. Harsher conditions prevailed more in the cotton belt than in the Upper South. But despite individual or regional variations, the system rested on the slave owner's absolute power, reinforced by the state.

Still, slave families and communities preserved their humanity in a system structured to destroy it. Slave religion, blending African spirituality with Islamic and Christian elements, proved crucial. Songs and folk tales mocked the master and celebrated slaves' ingenuity. Allusions in Christian hymnody to the Jews' escape from Egypt to "the promised land" expressed longings for freedom.

Subtle forms of resistance included breaking tools and slowing the work pace. Such action brought whippings, but the silent struggle continued. More daring slaves ran away. Those who reached the North found a network of safe houses, dubbed the "Underground Railroad" to speed them to Canada and freedom. Maryland's Harriet Tubman returned numerous times after her own escape in 1849 to bring out family members and others. Slave owners advertised rewards for runaways and harshly punished those who were caught. But the dashes to freedom continued, particularly from the Upper South. Young Frederick Douglass, escaping from Baltimore in 1838, joined the antislavery cause and wrote a popular autobiography.

Open rebellion constituted the most desperate if infrequent form of resistance. Denmark Vesey led a Charleston uprising in 1822, and Nat Turner another in Virginia in 1831. A lay preacher, Turner experienced visions directing him to organize resistance. He and a band of co-conspirators attacked local plantations, killing fifty-nine people. Brutal retribution followed, as terrified whites killed local slaves indiscriminately. Turner, captured after two months in hiding, was tried and hanged. In the aftermath, Virginia and other states adopted draconian slave codes enforcing the system even more severely.

The politics of slavery

Slavery presented a tangle of legal and political problems, often focused on the admission of new states. By 1819 the United States had an equal number of free and slave states, but even despite the

Constitution's three-fifths rule (by which three-fifths of each state's slave population was counted in determining its congressional delegation), the slave states had significantly fewer congressional members. When Missouri applied for statehood that year, southern politicians insisted that slavery be permitted. In 1820 Congress admitted Missouri as a slave state, balanced by free-state Maine. As part of the compromise, however, Congress prohibited slavery in the rest of the Louisiana Purchase north of the line 36° 30″, Missouri's southern boundary. The debate, wrote the aged Thomas Jefferson, alarmed him like "a fire bell in the night."

Bearing out Jefferson's apprehensions, slavery increasingly dominated national politics. In 1836, southern congressmen rammed through procedural rules barring Congress from receiving antislavery petitions. Former president John Quincy Adams, now in Congress, defended the constitutional right of petition, but the "gag rule" remained in force for eight years. In 1844 the presidential candidate of the antislavery Liberty Party (founded 1839) received 62,000 votes, enough to help Democrat James Polk defeat the Whig Henry Clay. Texas's admission as a slave state in 1845 deepened northern uneasiness. In 1847 the House of Representatives passed a bill banning slavery in territories acquired in the Mexican War, but the Senate rejected it. In 1848, the presidential candidate of the Free Soil Party, formed by dissident northern Whigs and Democrats opposed to slavery expansion, received 11 percent of the vote—further underscoring the issue's divisive potential.

This set the stage for the Compromise of 1850, a series of measures intended to defuse the controversy. While admitting California as a free state, Congress empowered the voters of New Mexico and Utah territories to decide the question themselves. While closing Washington's open-air slave market, Congress permitted slavery to continue in the nation's capital. In a major victory for the South, Congress enacted a harsh Fugitive Slave Law authorizing federal marshals, aided if necessary by deputized passersby, to seize escaped slaves and ship them South without a jury trial. To many northerners, this law underscored the truly implacable nature of "the Slave Power."

Debating slavery: from colonization to abolitionism

In the early national era, many southern leaders favored emancipating slaves and returning them to Africa. To achieve these goals, Robert Finley, a Presbyterian clergyman, founded the American Colonization Society (ACS) in 1816. Beginning in 1822, the ACS repatriated some 12,000 freed slaves to a West African coastal town they called Monrovia (for President James Monroe, an ACS supporter). From this settlement eventually emerged the nation of Liberia. By the 1830s, however, with cotton plantations expanding and attitudes hardening after Nat Turner's uprising, southern support for emancipation and colonization faded.

Many northerners, meanwhile, including recent immigrants, initially seemed willing to tolerate slavery, if confined to the South. Urban workers feared job competition if freed slaves migrated north. Textile mill owners and employees, dependent on southern cotton, had little incentive to oppose slavery. As slavery spread, however, threatening competition with free agriculture, opposition to expansion, if not to slavery itself, intensified. At the same time, the ranks of northerners who found slavery morally repugnant slowly grew. Quakers, honoring each person's spark of divinity, led the way. The British antislavery movement, culminating in 1833 with the abolition of slavery throughout the empire, resonated in America as well.

Antislavery advocates initially endorsed gradual emancipation with compensation to slave owners, but the 1830s brought demands for immediate abolition. Boston's William Lloyd Garrison, launching his periodical *The Liberator* in 1831, proclaimed: "I will not retreat a single inch. AND I WILL BE HEARD." In 1833 Garrison helped found the American

Antislavery Society. A thoroughgoing radical, he opposed political compromises and denounced the Constitution as "an agreement with hell." If slavery persisted in America, he insisted, the North must leave the union. As a pacifist, however, Garrison favored "moral suasion" as the way to eradicate the evil. Many reform-minded northern Protestants embraced abolitionism. Theodore Weld, a Presbyterian evangelist, organized abolitionist societies and, with his wife, Angelina Grimké Weld, compiled *American Slavery as It Is* (1839) from southern newspaper clippings.

Along with Frederick Douglass, other African Americans emerged as leaders. While the escaped slave William Wells Brown favored Garrison's "moral suasion" strategy, Henry Highland Garnet, another fugitive slave, was more militant. Addressing a National Negro Convention in Buffalo in 1843, Garnet praised Nat Turner and urged resistance by "every means . . . , moral, intellectual, and physical, that promises success." These tactical differences would resurface more than a century later, in the 1960s' black-freedom struggle.

Women figured prominently in the movement. The Grimké sisters, Sarah and Angelina, of a South Carolina slaveholding family, converted to Quakerism, moved to Philadelphia, and joined the cause. When New England ministers opposed their public lectures, they added women's rights to their reform agenda. Elizabeth Cady Stanton and Susan B. Anthony similarly combined antislavery and feminism when male leaders tried to marginalize them.

As abolitionism spread, opposition hardened. In 1835 a Boston mob nearly lynched Garrison, and a Charleston mob burned abolitionist literature stolen from the post office. The abolitionist editor Elijah Lovejoy was murdered in Alton, Illinois, in 1837. Across the North, mobs, some led by prominent citizens, disrupted abolitionist gatherings. In 1844–45, foreshadowing the secession crisis, southern Methodists and Baptists broke with their national religious bodies and formed separate denominations.

Hopes that the Compromise of 1850 would end the controversy quickly faded. In 1852, galvanized by the Fugitive Slave Act, Harriet Beecher Stowe, daughter of an evangelical minister, published *Uncle Tom's Cabin*, an antislavery novel appealing to middle-class moral sentiments in a sentimental age. Slavery destroys families, deadens human sympathy, and tramples Christian ethics, Stowe argued. An instant best seller across the North, the book's impact matched that of Tom Paine's *Common Sense* in 1776. Vivid scenes from Stowe's novel—Simon Legree brutally whipping the devoutly Christian slave Uncle Tom; Eliza bravely escaping to freedom across the frozen Ohio River— embedded themselves in the consciousness of a generation.

Southern writers answered with novels portraying happy slaves such as Mary Eastman's *Aunt Phillis's Cabin* (1852). In *Types of Mankind* (1854), the Alabama physician Josiah Nott proclaimed blacks' innate inferiority and endorsed polygenesis, the theory that they constituted a distinct, nonhuman species. Southern evangelicals rejected polygenesis, since it contradicted the Bible's creation story. Instead, they quoted biblical passages that seemed to approve of slavery. Taking a different tack, Virginia's George Fitzhugh, in *Sociology for the South* (1854), contrasted southern "family slavery" with capitalist "wage slavery." While benevolent masters watched over their slaves' welfare, Fitzhugh contended, northern factory owners ruthlessly exploited their workers. Despite his fanciful account of slavery, Fitzhugh's portrayal of northern factory conditions hit home.

On the political front, the anti-immigrant American Party briefly surged in 1854–55 as the Democratic and Whig parties fragmented. In the Kansas-Nebraska Act (May 1854), Congress adopted the "popular sovereignty" panacea of Senator Stephen Douglas, an Illinois Democrat. This law, repudiating the Missouri Compromise's ban on slavery north of latitude 36° 30″, empowered settlers in Kansas and Nebraska territories to determine by referendum whether to permit slavery. That July, northern Whig and Free Soil party leaders, meeting in Ripon, Wisconsin, formed a new political organization, the Republican Party, opposed to slavery expansion.

Douglas's "popular sovereignty" formula unleashed violence in Kansas as proslavery settlers from Missouri and northern antislavery settlers, some financed and armed by abolitionists, formed rival territorial governments and applied for statehood. On May 21, 1856, proslavery invaders from Missouri pillaged Lawrence, Kansas, an antislavery stronghold. Three days later, the abolitionist John Brown, with four of his sons and two other men, massacred five proslavery settlers in Pottawatomie, Kansas. All told, guerrilla fighting in "Bleeding Kansas" left some two hundred dead. (After complicated political maneuvering, Kansas entered the union as a free state in 1861.) Back in Washington that eventful May, the Massachusetts senator Charles Sumner stridently denounced the "slave oligarchy" in a three-hour harangue. Two days later, the South Carolina congressman Preston Brooks viciously attacked Sumner with a heavy cane, leaving him bleeding and unconscious on the Senate floor. Southern admirers deluged Brooks with replacement canes.

The Pennsylvania Democrat James Buchanan, with southern support, won the 1856 presidential election. But the Republican candidate John C. Frémont, a celebrated explorer, carried eleven northern states, signaling both the new party's strength and its limited regional base. Buchanan's inaugural address attacking abolitionism and opposing any federal ban on slavery in the territories dismayed antislavery northerners.

So did the Supreme Court's 1857 *Dred Scott* decision. Scott, a slave, sued for freedom on the grounds that his former owner, an army surgeon, had taken him to the free territories of Illinois and Wisconsin. Led by Chief Justice Roger Taney of Maryland, the court rejected Scott's claim, 7–2, holding that slaves were not citizens and had no right to sue. The majority further declared the

Missouri Compromise unconstitutional, since its ban on slavery in the northern territories denied slave owners' property rights without due process of law. Surveying these events, the New York senator William Seward grimly foresaw an "irrepressible conflict" ahead.

In 1858, Illinois Republicans nominated the lawyer Abraham Lincoln to challenge Stephen Douglas for his U.S. Senate seat. In a series of debates, Lincoln targeted Douglas's "popular sovereignty" idea. Under the *Dred Scott* ruling, he asked, how could the residents of *any* territory ban slavery? They could do so, Douglas cagily responded, by withholding the enforcement regulations that slavery required—an answer that angered slavery defenders. Douglas won, but Lincoln gained national visibility.

In October 1859 John Brown, secretly backed by prominent abolitionists, led eighteen men, including five blacks, in a raid on the U.S. arsenal at Harpers Ferry, Virginia. He planned to arm local slaves, triggering a wider uprising. Federal troops under Robert E. Lee easily captured the raiders, and Brown and six of his band were tried and hanged. Soon, northern troops would march to war singing, "John Brown's body lies a-mouldering in the grave, but his truth goes marching on."

Speaking in New York City in February 1860, Abraham Lincoln condemned abolitionist extremism but insisted that slavery expansion must stop. In a contemptuous response, the Senate in May passed resolutions proposed by South Carolina's Jefferson Davis denying the government's power to ban slavery anywhere, and, indeed, asserting its duty to support slavery throughout the territories.

In May, the Republican convention in Chicago nominated Lincoln for president. As the Whig Party essentially collapsed and the Democrats' northern and southern wings nominated separate candidates, Lincoln won with a 40 percent plurality. Ominously, however, he carried the Electoral College without a single southern vote.

The South quickly reacted. In December, amid cheers and fireworks, a convention in Charleston, South Carolina, proclaimed: "[T]he Union subsisting between South Carolina and other States, under the name of the United States of America, is hereby dissolved." By February 1861, eleven southern states had seceded and formed the Confederate States of America under President Jefferson Davis. "We are divorced, North from South," wrote South Carolina's Mary Boykin Chesnut in her diary, "because we hated each other so."

Some southern apologists would later claim that differing constitutional interpretations of states' rights caused the Civil War. In fact, South Carolina's secession proclamation explicitly stated the cause: the election of a president "whose opinions and purposes are hostile to slavery." From the first, the issue at stake was the South's determination to perpetuate slavery.

President Buchanan remained passively aloof as southern troops occupied federal forts. He ordered a supply ship to Fort Sumter in Charleston harbor, but it withdrew after encountering shore fire. In his March 4, 1861, inaugural address, Lincoln offered conciliatory words, pledged not to disturb slavery where it existed but vowed to resist secession. On April 12, when Fort Sumter's commander refused to surrender, shore batteries opened fire. Declaring a national insurrection, Lincoln called for 75,000 volunteers. Seward's "irrepressible conflict" had come.

Civil War

The North enjoyed advantages in technology, transportation, finance, and population (22 million versus the South's 9 million, including 3.5 million slaves). Confederate leaders hoped for British support, given cotton's importance to England's textile industry.

But British opinion was divided, and Washington warned London against interfering. Despite strains in U.S.-British relations, London never recognized the Confederacy.

Northern hopes for a quick victory in the East evaporated in July 1861 after a Union defeat at Bull Run (First Manassas battle) near Washington, and the war on the eastern front settled into stalemate. Union general George McClellan, invading Virginia via Chesapeake Bay in March 1862, approached Richmond, the Confederate capital, but retreated after fierce fighting. In a fall 1862 offensive targeting Washington, Confederate generals Robert E. Lee and Thomas "Stonewall" Jackson advanced through Maryland. McClellan stopped them at Antietam on September 17, the war's bloodiest day, but failed to pursue his advantage. Frustrated, Lincoln tried a succession of generals, but the stalemate continued.

Elsewhere, U.S. naval forces did better, occupying New Orleans (April 1862) and blockading Confederate shipping. In the West, Union general Ulysses S. Grant captured key forts in northern Tennessee early in 1862, and in April, aided by troops under General Don Carlos Buell, defeated the Confederates at Shiloh near Corinth, Mississippi, both sides suffering heavy casualties. A Confederate defeat at Murfreesboro (January 1863) assured Union control of central Tennessee. After a long siege, Grant took Vicksburg, a Confederate stronghold on the Mississippi, on July 4, 1863, and Chattanooga, a rail and communications hub, fell in November, effectively ending the war in the West.

After Confederate victories in Virginia at Fredericksburg (December 1862) and Chancellorsville (May 1863), Lee again marched north. At Gettysburg, Pennsylvania (July 1–4, 1863), in the war's turning point, Union forces repelled his advance. That November, dedicating a Union cemetery at Gettysburg, Lincoln honored those who had given their lives so that "government of the people, by the people, and for the people shall not perish from the earth." Only 272 words long, Lincoln's Gettysburg Address ranks among the greatest of presidential speeches.

In March 1864, Grant, now commanding all Union armies, invaded Virginia. Battles at Spotsylvania, Cold Harbor, and Petersburg took a terrible toll, but Grant grimly pushed on toward Richmond. General William T. Sherman captured Atlanta in September (aiding Lincoln's reelection bid) and marched eastward to Savannah, leaving devastation in his wake. On April 9, 1865, at Appomattox Court House in Virginia, Lee surrendered. At a cost of more than 617,000 dead on both sides (of a total population of 31.4 million), the United States survived.

Lincoln had little time to savor victory. On April 15, at Washington's Ford's Theatre, the actor John Wilkes Booth, a Confederate sympathizer, shot him. Death came the following day.

4. **Confederate dead at Gettysburg, July 5, 1863. As Civil War photographers went into the field of combat, they brought home to the civilian population the horrifying reality of mass slaughter.**

The war, slavery, and African Americans

Lincoln went to war to save the Union, not to end slavery. While personally opposed to slavery, he presided over a divided cabinet and nation, including three slave states that remained in the Union: Maryland, Kentucky, and Missouri. Nevertheless, emancipation gradually emerged as a war aim, reflecting both abolitionist pressure and the many escaped slaves (eventually reaching half a million) who fled to Union camps and aided the war effort.

In September 1862, after the battle at Antietam, Lincoln issued the Emancipation Proclamation, freeing slaves in areas captured by Union troops. A Union victory, in short, meant near-universal emancipation. Reversing earlier policy, the administration now welcomed African Americans into the military. By war's end, 186,000 had served, in segregated units under white officers. Although mostly assigned non-combat duties, blacks fought in several engagements, notably a July 1863 assault on Fort Wagner, South Carolina. Even slaves who remained with their masters employed subtle stratagems that weakened the Confederacy's economy.

The war at home

Volunteers on both sides, especially women, supported the war effort, managing plantations and farms in the absence of husbands and sons. Northern women organized "Sanitary Fairs" to raise funds for the U.S. Sanitary Commission, a voluntary organization that aided the troops by supplying needed medical and sanitary supplies. Other women volunteers transported food to the troops to supplement army rations. More than three thousand women on both sides served as voluntary nurses. Among them was a patent-office clerk, Clara Barton, who would later found the United States Red Cross. The poet Walt Whitman volunteered as a hospital aide in Washington, DC, recording his impressions in *Drum-Taps* (1865) and other works.

The war also stirred opposition in the North. When Congress imposed a draft in 1863, poor Irish immigrants rioted. (The rich could avoid the draft by hiring a substitute.) In New York City, rioters targeted draft offices and prominent Republicans' residences and lynched several African Americans before federal troops restored order. Clamping down on opposition, Lincoln in 1863 suspended the writ of habeas corpus, approving the arrest (most only briefly) of some 15,000 Confederate sympathizers and war critics. This policy would be cited as a precedent for repressing dissent in future wars.

Reconstruction's failed promise

The Thirteenth Amendment (1865) ended slavery, but southern legislatures enacted "Black Codes" restricting freedmen's rights and imposing labor rules little different from slavery. In response, Republicans in Congress extended the wartime Freedmen's Bureau created to protect ex-slaves; passed a Civil Rights Act overriding the Black Codes; and adopted the Fourteenth Amendment (1868) guaranteeing citizenship and equal rights to all persons born or naturalized in the United States (except Indians). Defying Congress, Lincoln's successor, Andrew Johnson of Tennessee, opposed these measures. (Impeached in 1868 in a conflict over presidential appointment powers, Johnson narrowly escaped removal from office.)

Reversing Johnson's lenient policies, Congress in 1867 placed the South under military rule. To reenter the Union, ex-Confederate states now had to ratify the Fourteenth Amendment and guarantee freedmen's rights. During this period, known as Radical Reconstruction, southern blacks served in state legislatures and several went to Congress, including two senators from Mississippi. Despite instances of corruption (exaggerated by critics), Reconstruction legislatures financed public education, hospitals, and asylums, and adopted measures protecting freedmen's rights.

In 1868 the Republican Ulysses Grant, running on a platform supporting Radical Reconstruction, won the presidency, aided by southern black voters. The Fifteenth Amendment (1870) forbade the denial of any citizen's voting rights because of "race, color, or previous condition of servitude." (The amendment disappointed feminists hoping it would also enfranchise women.)

Radical Reconstruction produced a powerful backlash. In 1865 Confederate veterans formed the secretive Ku Klux Klan, which terrorized black voters and Republican politicians, white and black, across the South. In Louisiana, Klansmen and other terrorists murdered hundreds in a campaign of intimidation.

The 1875 Civil Rights Act granted all persons equal access to public places and conveyances. But northern support for Reconstruction was weakening, particularly when an economic depression hit in 1873. In 1876 the Democratic presidential candidate, New York governor Samuel Tilden, won the popular vote, but the Electoral College tally was disputed. In the ensuing bargaining in the House of Representatives, southerners agreed to support the Republican Rutherford B. Hayes for president in return for various concessions, including the end of military rule in the South. As federal troops withdrew, white supremacists regained control.

By 1877 slavery had been abolished and (on paper) freedmen enjoyed full citizenship rights. By the 1890s, however, resurgent white racism reversed these gains. Across the South, officials imposed racial segregation and thwarted black voters by various devious tactics. Discrimination pervaded the North as well. Much had changed on the racial front. But as white America's attention turned elsewhere, much remained the same.

Chapter 5
1866–1900: Industrialization and its consequences

On May 10, 1869, at Promontory Point, Utah, workers drove a spike that linked two rail lines, one snaking from the East, the other from California, completing America's first transcontinental railroad. This event helped launch an era of economic development that would transform a Jeffersonian society of yeoman farmers into an industrial powerhouse.

Industrialization unleashed profound social changes, as bankers and corporate managers, factory laborers and clerical workers, crowded the nation's cities, and immigrants arrived by the millions. As a new capitalist elite flaunted its wealth and political clout, class divisions sharpened and Lincoln's vision of government "of the people, by the people, and for the people" seemed quaintly idealistic. Belying the promise of the Civil War era, these decades saw an ugly upsurge of racism. While some writers and social thinkers saw America's laissez-faire capitalist system as the path to progress, others viewed the new order with profound uneasiness.

The new industrial order

Post–Civil War industrialization required raw materials, an expanding labor force, governmental support, and technological innovations in such basic industries as steel, railroads, steam and electric power, and petroleum. New corporate structures and financial institutions proved crucial as well. Powerful captains of industry, with their wealth, political influence, and cultural resonance, set the tone of American life in these years.

At midcentury, America's iron industry consisted of numerous small-scale mines and smelting facilities. In the 1870s the Scottish immigrant Andrew Carnegie, having risen through the ranks of the Pennsylvania Railroad, acquired mines, mills, and shipping facilities, and welded them into a corporate giant, the Carnegie Steel Company. Transporting ore by water and rail from Minnesota's Mesabi range, Carnegie refined it at his plant near Pittsburgh, creating a vertically integrated production chain from iron mine to finished steel. Adopting the Bessemer process, a technique for removing impurities from molten iron through oxidation, Carnegie mass-produced high-quality steel for the nation's railroads, steam turbines, machine shops, and farm-equipment manufacturers. By 1890 U.S. steel production surpassed Great Britain's—a symbolic moment in America's industrial rise.

America's railroad network already comprised 30,000 miles of track by 1860, and the postwar years brought still more rapid expansion. Amid cut-throat competition, political chicanery, and frenzied construction booms, railroad ventures sprouted like mushrooms and sometimes collapsed spectacularly. By 1900 America boasted some 200,000 miles of track and the industry was capitalized at nearly $10 billion—more than $260 billion in today's buying power.

Railroads undergirded the nation's postwar economic boom, transporting coal and iron ore to Carnegie's steel mills, farm equipment to rural America, livestock to Chicago's slaughterhouses, grain to the mills of Minneapolis, machinery and consumer goods across the land, and immigrants to the vast interior. Rail tycoons like Collis P. Huntington and Leland

5. A view inside Andrew Carnegie's cavernous steel works at Homestead, Pennsylvania, near Pittsburgh. Post–Civil War industrial expansion, typified by such factories, transformed the United States in many ways.

Stanford in California, Cornelius Vanderbilt and Jay Gould in New York, and James J. Hill in Minnesota were among the best known, and most feared, figures of the age.

Coal-fueled steam engines powered the era's factories, locomotives, machinery works, and grain mills. Steam technology developed rapidly in the late nineteenth century, powering ocean liners and industrial turbines At the 1876 Philadelphia Centennial Exposition, a 1,400-horsepower steam dynamo, 45 feet tall, with a 30-foot-diameter flywheel, manufactured by the Corliss Steam Engine Company of Providence, powered the exposition's machinery through a network of gears and shafts. The novelist William Dean Howells wrote in awe: "The Corliss engine does not lend itself to description; its personal acquaintance must be sought by those who would understand its vast and almost silent grandeur. It rises loftily in the centre of the huge structure, an athlete of steel and iron."

By 1900 electricity, generated at water-driven or coal-fueled plants, represented a new power source, freeing machines from fixed steam pipes and drive shafts. Thanks to Thomas Edison and other inventors, these years brought not only electrified machinery but also streetcars and street lights. As in the steel business, large firms swallowed smaller ones, and two corporations, General Electric and Westinghouse, soon dominated the industry.

All this machinery needed lubrication, and a burgeoning petroleum industry supplied it. The nation's first oil well gushed into life in 1859 in western Pennsylvania. More followed, and soon the United States ranked first in world oil production. Once again, consolidation replaced chaotic competition. Ruthlessly strangling smaller entrepreneurs, John D. Rockefeller's Standard Oil Company (incorporated 1867) soon controlled the oil refining business by a process of dominance called "horizontal integration."

An expanding financial system provided the capital for this burst of industrialization. American and foreign investment banks not only marketed the stock and bond offerings of the great corporations but also directed their development. J. P. Morgan's New York City bank, with branches in London and Paris, controlled several railroads and arranged many of the era's biggest corporate consolidations. In 1901 Morgan bought out Andrew Carnegie and founded the United States Steel Company. A year later he created the International Harvester Company, a farm-equipment conglomerate. On several occasions, Morgan even helped the U.S. Treasury weather financial crises.

The social cost of industrialization

Industrialization had an impact on American life at all levels, as eager workers poured into the nation's industrial centers. In 1850 the United States was an agrarian society with some towns and cities; by 1900 it was an urban-industrial nation with a strong agricultural hinterland. New York City's 1900 population of 3.4 million approximated America's *total* urban population in 1850.

Many urban newcomers came from America's farms and small towns, but millions more arrived from Europe, pushed by deprivation at home and pulled by hopes of a better life in America. By 1900 the U.S. population was 20 percent foreign born, with far higher percentages in the big industrial cities. In contrast to earlier waves of immigration from Great Britain, Ireland, Germany, and Scandinavia, these newer immigrants came mainly from southern and eastern Europe—Italy, Greece, Poland, Russia, the Balkans—with the Catholic, Jewish, and Orthodox Christian faiths heavily represented. These demographic shifts contained the seeds of ethnic tensions, cultural diversity, and political realignments.

While many settled on western farms, thousands more took jobs in the factories, mills, and railroad yards of Cleveland, Pittsburgh, St. Louis, Chicago, Milwaukee, Minneapolis, and other industrial centers. Cities reeled as explosive growth strained housing, schools, transportation, and municipal services. Tuberculosis, typhoid fever, and other diseases took a fearful toll in teeming, unsanitary immigrant slums like those in New York's Lower East Side, as impoverished newcomers crowded into unhealthful tenements. In 1870 more than 20 percent of babies born in New York City died in infancy. Churches, synagogues, and city missions offered the consolations of religion, while a vibrant popular culture of variety theaters, dance halls, saloons, and amusement parks provided immigrants at least temporary escape from the stresses and hazards of their new life.

The urban poor stirred both compassion and fear among the middle class. The photo-journalist Jacob Riis vividly evoked slum life in *How the Other Half Lives* (1890). Reformers like Chicago's Jane Addams opened settlement houses to provide social services and build bonds of sympathy between the newcomers and middle-class volunteers.

Urban political machines supplied municipal services and jobs to immigrants, but often at the price of corruption. New York City's government under William M. ("Boss") Tweed was so notoriously larcenous that a wave of outraged reform by "the wisest and best citizens," fueled by exposés in the *New York Times* and satirical cartoons in *Harper's Weekly*, landed Tweed in prison in 1873.

Factories, mills, and railroads offered jobs, but at a heavy social cost. Work was exhausting, hours long, wages low, conditions

THE "BRAINS"
THAT ACHIEVED THE TAMMANY VICTORY AT THE ROCHESTER DEMOCRATIC CONVENTION.

6. New York's political boss, William M. Tweed, as caricatured in 1871 by cartoonist Thomas Nast. Many U.S. cities, overwhelmed by rapid growth, were dominated by corrupt politicians in the late nineteenth century, leading to a wave of municipal reform campaigns.

dangerous, and vacations unknown. Frequent accidents devastated workers' families. In 1890, 2,451 railroad workers were killed on the job, and more than twenty-two thousand injured. A few big employers adopted a paternalistic approach. George Pullman, owner of a railway sleeping-car factory near Chicago, provided his workers housing and cultural amenities, while barring alcohol and otherwise regulating their behavior. Most capitalists, however, cared little about their workers, who were easily replaceable. In a boom-and-bust economy, downturns resulted in layoffs and wage cuts. A severe depression in 1893–97 caused terrible suffering. In Chicago, desperate people scrounged in garbage dumps for food.

Such conditions triggered labor unrest, violence, and unionization efforts. In 1877 rail workers protesting wage cuts walked off the job nationwide. Meanwhile, the Knights of Labor, founded by Philadelphia garment workers in 1869, envisioned a union of all workers, irrespective of race or gender. It grew rapidly, and in 1884–85 won a strike against Jay Gould's Wabash railroad. Fearing job competition, the Knights favored immigration restriction, especially of Chinese on the West Coast. Partially through their efforts, Congress passed the Chinese Exclusion Act (1882), which remained in effect until 1943.

Skilled craft unions such as cigar makers, printers, and machinists disliked the Knights' all-inclusive approach, and in 1886 a group of craft unions founded the American Federation of Labor (AFL). Under Samuel Gompers, the AFL accepted the capitalist system, focusing instead on higher wages and immigration restriction. On May Day, 1886, in an action coordinated by various labor and radical organizations, workers in major cities went on strike demanding an eight-hour work day. On May 3, at Chicago's International Harvester Company, two strikers died under a hail of police gunfire. An anarchist-sponsored protest rally the following evening in Chicago's Haymarket Square was breaking up when the police suddenly waded in. Someone threw an explosive device, killing a policeman. In the chaotic aftermath, four protesters and seven more policemen died, most from panicky police gunfire. The "Haymarket massacre" terrified wealthy and middle-class Americans. A religious paper, the *Congregationalist*, declared: "When anarchy gathers its deluded disciples into a mob, as at Chicago, a Gatling gun or two . . . offers, on the whole, the most merciful as well as effectual remedy." Eight Chicago anarchists were arrested and tried. Though prosecutors proved no connection to the bomb-thrower, four were hanged and one committed suicide. In 1893 the Illinois governor John P. Altgeld, a labor sympathizer, commuted the sentences of the remaining three. He lost the next election.

In 1892 officials at Carnegie's steel mill near Pittsburgh locked out workers trying to organize a union, and brought in three hundred agents of the Pinkerton Detective Agency to protect strikebreakers hired to replace them (called "scabs" by the strikers). Gunfire erupted, killing three Pinkerton agents and seven workers. National guardsmen mobilized by Pennsylvania's governor broke the strike. Two years later, when Pullman workers struck, protesting wage cuts, the American Railway Union declared a national sympathy strike. The U.S. attorney general, declaring the nation "on the ragged edge of anarchy," secured a court injunction to break the strike and jail the union president, Eugene V. Debs. (Converted to socialism in prison, Debs later ran for president on the Socialist Party ticket.)

Despite fierce opposition from the corporate and governmental power elites, unionization continued. But with the Knights of Labor fading and the AFL limited to the skilled trades, most factory workers remained unorganized, at the mercy of their employers.

Politics in a corporate age

The interests of workers, consumers, and the urban poor drew scant attention in the halls of power, as politicians at all levels served the corporate interests. Sometimes money changed hands, but the ideology and class interests of the business and political elites were so nearly indistinguishable that bribery often proved unnecessary. The government subsidized railroad construction, enacted high protective tariffs, and forcibly put down striking workers. One regulatory reform did gain traction: an "antitrust" movement reflecting fears that corporate consolidation, epitomized by the Standard Oil Trust (1879), was stifling competition. The Sherman Antitrust Act (1890) outlawed "conspiracies in restraint of trade," but enforcement was sporadic. Indeed, the first significant prosecution, in 1894, was against a labor organization: Eugene Debs' American Railway Union.

Other issues periodically arose, of course. Congress granted generous benefits to Union Army veterans, a politically powerful lobby. And in 1883, after a disappointed and deranged office seeker assassinated President James A. Garfield, Congress passed a civil-service act requiring that some government jobs be filled by examination rather than by patronage appointment.

The era's one major anticorporate political movement mobilized not industrial workers or the urban poor, but debt-ridden wheat and cotton farmers on the Great Plains and in the South battered by falling commodity prices, tight credit, discriminatory railroad rates, and high farm-equipment prices. In the 1880s, southern and western Farmers' Alliance movements formed cooperatives to increase their commodity-marketing power and bargaining clout with railroads, equipment dealers, and mill operators. More radical alliance leaders advocated government regulation to lower railroad rates and force eastern bankers to ease their credit practices.

In 1892 the presidential candidate of the new Populist Party received more than a million votes and carried four western states. In 1896, as debt, drought, and depression took their toll, the Populists fused with the Democratic Party, adopting a platform incorporating the Farmers' Alliance reforms and adding the unlimited coinage of silver to increase the money supply in the West—a reform backed by western silver-mine owners. The fusion candidate, Nebraska's William Jennings Bryan, received 6.4 million votes but attracted few industrial workers, who felt little in common with protesting farmers. The Republican candidate, William McKinley, won handily with heavy financial backing from the nation's corporate and financial elites.

While these agrarian reformers energized the political process and recognized unregulated corporate power as an urgent issue, they represented a single economic interest group, and failed to attract urban workers or consumers. Not until the 1930s would Franklin D. Roosevelt forge a reform alliance including farmers and industrial workers.

African Americans and women in the late nineteenth century

African Americans, residing mostly in the South, many as tenant farmers and sharecroppers, faced blatant racism and voting discrimination. The South's ruling Democratic Party firmly upheld white supremacy. Booker T. Washington's Tuskegee Institute in Alabama and a few other schools offered black youth vocational training, but within a rigid racial hierarchy. Northern blacks, confined by custom to urban "colored districts," worked in low-paying menial jobs or specific occupations such as barbers or railroad porters.

The federal government acquiesced in this racial caste system. Indeed, in *Plessy v. Ferguson* (1896), the U.S. Supreme Court, by a 7–1 vote, upheld an 1890 Louisiana statute requiring railroads to provide "equal, but separate, accommodations for the white and colored races." The court rejected the plaintiff's claim that this violated the Fourteenth Amendment's guarantee of "equal protection of the law" to all. After *Plessy*, racial segregation was even more rigidly enforced. The one bright spot in this shameful decision was a stinging dissent by John Marshall Harlan of Kentucky, himself a former slave owner. Wrote Harlan: "Our constitution is color-blind. . . . In respect of civil rights, all citizens are equal before the law. The humblest is the peer of the most powerful. . . . The thin disguise of 'equal' accommodations for passengers in railroad coaches will not mislead anyone, nor atone for the wrong this day done."

Even at this low point, a few black leaders fearlessly protested racism. The journalist Ida B. Wells, driven from Memphis in 1892 when a mob destroyed her newspaper offices after she denounced lynchings in the city, published *The Red Record* (1895), documenting the terrorism by which white racists intimidated black communities.

Women's situation varied widely, depending on geography, race, ethnicity, and class. African American women faced double discrimination, both racial and gender. Farm wives, amid child-rearing, housekeeping, and chores, often battled loneliness, especially on the Great Plains. The Farmers' Alliance and Populist movements provided social outlets and, for some, a public voice. Mary Lease of Kansas, a fiery Populist orator, urged farmers to "raise less corn and more hell."

In the cities, upper-class women enjoyed lives of leisured privilege. Immigrant women, by contrast, found life exceedingly harsh. Some supplemented their meager family income as domestic servants or garment workers in sweatshops. Among the growing ranks of middle-class women, some sought college education and pursued careers as teachers, librarians, nurses, clerical workers, or clerks in department stores like Macy's in New York City. A burgeoning women's-club movement offered social support and cultural enrichment, while settlement houses and the Charity Organization movement (whose "Friendly Visitors" preached sobriety and thrift to the immigrant poor) provided volunteer opportunities. Despite widespread cultural assumptions that saw the domestic sphere as women's proper domain, city life opened new vistas, and veteran feminists like Elizabeth Cady Stanton and

Susan B. Anthony carried on the battle for the vote and equality, laying the groundwork for future progress.

Writers and thinkers assess the new order

Tycoons like Rockefeller, Huntington, and Morgan put their imprint on the age, inspiring hatred, hostility, and sometimes grudging admiration. Some endowed libraries, orchestras, and other cultural institutions; others acquired vast art collections that would eventually make their way into museums. Andrew Carnegie's rise from poverty became the prototype for a rags-to-riches mythology purveyed by popular writers like Horatio Alger, whose *Ragged Dick* (1867) and other tales preached upward mobility through honesty, frugality—and improbable strokes of luck.

Some social thinkers welcomed the brutally competitive new order. As early as 1850, the British sociologist Herbert Spencer argued that the competitive struggle assured "the survival of the fittest." In his study *On the Origin of Species* (1859), Charles Darwin viewed competition in the natural world, aided by natural selection—the chance variations that increase some individuals' prospects to survive and reproduce—as the mechanism of evolutionary change. The Yale sociologist William Graham Sumner saw the same process at work in human society, with unbridled competition assuring social progress, provided government and reformers kept their hands off. To aid society's losers simply assured the survival of the unfit. "A drunkard in the gutter is just where he ought to be," Sumner memorably declared; "[undergoing] the process of . . . dissolution by which [nature] removes things which have survived their usefulness."

Challenging this callous version of Social Darwinism, Lester Ward in *Dynamic Sociology* (1883) argued that the relevant evolutionary unit was not the individual but society itself. Societies progress not by maximizing competition and abandoning the "losers" to their fate, Ward contended, but by fostering the well-being of all, including the weak and destitute.

Offering a cultural appraisal in their 1873 novel *The Gilded Age*, Mark Twain and Charles Dudley Warner found post–Civil War society tawdry and gross. The economist Thorstein Veblen in *The Theory of the Leisure Class* (1899) probed the "conspicuous consumption" by which the rich flaunted their wealth and asserted their supposed superiority. William Dean Howells's *The Rise of Silas Lapham* (1885) portrayed the efforts of a nouveau riche paint tycoon to break into Boston society even as brutal competitive pressures drive him to bankruptcy. And Frank Norris in *The Octopus* (1901) offered a thinly fictionalized account of the ruthlessness with which California railroad magnates crushed the farmers who challenged them.

Other writers explored the situation of women, of all social ranks, in an urban-industrial age. In *Maggie: A Girl of the Streets* (1896), Stephen Crane pictured an innocent slum girl's seduction and fall into prostitution. In *The Awakening* (1899), by the New Orleans writer Kate Chopin, a bored leisure-class woman is ostracized and ultimately driven to suicide when she flouts the sexual proprieties of her social class. Charlotte Perkins Gilman's short story "The Yellow Wall-Paper" (1892), drawn from her own experience, told of a pampered young wife's vacuous existence and eventual mental breakdown. In *Women and Economics* (1898), Gilman explored the historical origins of female subordination and its anachronistic perpetuation in the modern era. Cumulatively, all these works offered a bleak and sobering picture of what Mark Twain and his co-author called "the Gilded Age."

Imperial dreams and war with Spain

As industrialization proceeded, politicians, journalists, business leaders, and military strategists offered expansive visions of America's global role. With European nations acquiring colonies in Africa and Asia, U.S. corporate and agricultural interests looked abroad as well. The search for markets drove the expansionist impulse. Secretary of State James G. Blaine observed in 1890: "[T]he United States has . . . developed a volume of manufactures which . . . overruns the demands of the home market. . . . Our present demand is expansion."

In Hawaii in 1893, U.S. sugar planters, some descended from missionaries who had arrived in the 1820s, organized a coup, backed by U.S. marines, sailors, and a warship, that overthrew the country's monarch, Queen Lili'uokalani, and U.S. annexation followed in 1898. At the same time, closer to home, New York's tabloid newspapers, engaged in a fierce circulation battle, denounced Spain's harsh repression of rebels fighting Spanish rule in Cuba, where American investors had extensive sugar-plantation holdings. When the U.S. battleship *Maine* blew up in Havana harbor on February 15, 1898, killing 266 sailors, the jingoistic press immediately blamed Spain and demanded war. (The cause of the blast has never been clearly established.) President McKinley bowed to the pressure, and on April 20 Congress declared war. Spain's small Cuban garrison and outgunned fleet soon fell to U.S. naval and land forces (including a volunteer cavalry unit commanded by Colonel Theodore Roosevelt), with heavy Spanish casualties. More than five thousand American soldiers died, mainly from disease and food poisoning. Although Congress forbade formal annexation, this "splendid little war" (as one Washington diplomat described it) led to decades of U.S. economic and military domination of Cuba.

By terms of the 1898 peace treaty, in return for a payment of $20 million, Spain ceded to the United States Puerto Rico, Guam, and the Philippine islands, whose Spanish colonial administrators had surrendered after a U.S. naval fleet under Admiral George Dewey blockaded Manila. This led to a three-year war to defeat Filipino insurgents fighting for independence. The war cost more than four thousand American lives, and an estimated 200,000 Filipinos died, both soldiers and civilians caught up in the combat.

Just as the Mexican War roused opposition in the 1840s, this new expansionist surge stirred home front protest. A congressional committee heard testimony of torture of Filipino insurgents by U.S. troops, including a technique called waterboarding. An Anti-Imperialist League, including Jane Addams, Andrew Carnegie, Mark Twain, and the philosopher William James, passionately warned that imperialist expansion betrayed the nation's founding principles and marked a troubling new turn in America's role in the world.

Many Americans felt pride in the nation's post–Civil War economic transformation. And, indeed, industrialization held promise of material betterment. Yet in many ways its political, social, and international consequences proved disastrous, including exploited workers, dangerous factories, urban slums, extreme class divisions, and a political system subservient to the business class. For African Americans, pervasive racism mocked the gains of the Civil War era. For women, the impact of the new order was mixed at best. In 1900, after decades of industrialization, urban growth, and a growing U.S. presence abroad, some 40 percent of Americans lived in poverty, and U.S. troops were battling freedom fighters in the Philippines. If present trends continued, wrote the poet Walt Whitman in 1879, "then our republican experiment, notwithstanding all its surface successes, is at heart an unhealthy failure."

As a new century dawned, accumulating discontents with the direction of the national life would fuel a new surge of reformist energy.

Chapter 6
1900–1920: Reform and war

On Saturday, March 25, 1911, seamstresses on the upper floors of New York's Triangle Shirtwaist factory neared the end of a long work week. Suddenly fire erupted. With no extinguishers or fire escapes, and exit doors locked or opening inward (a fire-code violation), the workers, mostly young immigrant women, had little chance; 141 died, either in the inferno itself or in desperate leaps from the windows. The catastrophe sharpened public awareness of industrialization's human toll—an awareness that had been growing for years. By the late nineteenth century, the social consequences of industrialization and urbanization disturbed many thoughtful Americans, feeding a reformist surge that historians call the Progressive movement.

Meanwhile, in 1914, long-festering rivalries in Europe exploded into war. Initially proclaiming U.S. neutrality, President Woodrow Wilson eventually led America into the conflict. Inspired by Wilson's idealistic rhetoric, Americans responded with high resolve. The war also stirred currents of bigotry and fear, however, fueling a disillusioned postwar reaction.

Reform energies awaken

Already in the Gilded Age, unregulated corporate power, widening class disparities, and appalling conditions in factories and immigrant cities stirred concern. Reform-minded ministers,

7. Police officers collect the bodies of the victims of the 1911 Triangle Shirtwaist fire in New York City. This catastrophic blaze, which killed 141 young garment workers, shocked a nation into confronting the social and human toll of unregulated industrial expansion.

preaching what they called the Social Gospel, insisted that Jesus's teachings, if taken seriously, required concern for the poor and exploited. The British reformer William Stead challenged comfortable middle-class churchgoers to confront the grim underside of American life in *If Christ Came to Chicago* (1893). Charles Sheldon, a Congregationalist minister in Topeka, Kansas, did the same in his bestselling novel *In His Steps; What Would Jesus Do?* (1896). (Echoes of Sheldon's novel survive in contemporary "WWJD" bracelets, coffee cups, and bumper stickers.)

Some reformers focused on moral uplift. The Woman's Christian Temperance Union (1874) and the Anti-Saloon League (1895) campaigned to prohibit alcohol. Antiprostitution crusaders, invoking the abolitionist movement, urged the eradication of "white slavery" from America's cities. Others, however, drawing on reform initiatives in England, Germany, Australia, and elsewhere, advocated more radical solutions, including electoral reforms; support for labor unions; governmental regulation of corporate behavior; and legislation addressing unsafe factories, child labor, and unhealthful conditions in the immigrant cities. Some even embraced Socialism. Jane Addams in *Democracy and Society Ethics* (1902) drew on her settlement-house experiences to argue that "democracy" in an industrial age must encompass not only the right to vote but also public efforts to ameliorate the plight of society's most desperate and vulnerable members. The journalist Herbert Croly in *The Promise of American Life* (1909) renewed Alexander Hamilton's call for an activist government—but now in the interests of all, not just the business class.

Mass magazines like *McClure's* and *Colliers* publicized terrible conditions in urban-industrial America. These exposés often then appeared as books, extending their influence. Ida Tarbell documented John D. Rockefeller's ruthless tactics in her *History of the Standard Oil Company* (1904). David Graham Phillips described Big Business's stranglehold over politics in *The Treason of the Senate* (1906). John Spargo in *The Bitter Cry of the Children* (1906) wrote movingly of the 1.7 million children in the industrial labor force. Upton Sinclair's *The Jungle* (1906), an exposé of worker exploitation and disgusting conditions in Chicago's packing plants, awakened consumers to the dangers of tainted meat. "I aimed at the public's heart, and by accident I hit it in the stomach," Sinclair later recalled.

Mobilizing locally, reformers from New York to San Francisco battled municipal corruption, documented in Lincoln Steffens's *The Shame of the Cities* (1904). Sensing an opportunity, some business leaders proposed structural reforms, such as citywide rather than ward-based elections, and "city managers" rather than mayors, to increase corporate influence and reduce immigrants' political power. After decades of helter-skelter growth, city-planning and urban-beautification advocates won support. More beautiful cities would promote good citizenship, they argued.

Other local and state-level reforms concentrated on worker protection and business regulation, including factory safety standards, prohibitions on child labor, and curbing pollution from belching smokestacks. After the Triangle fire, New York State enacted numerous worker-protection laws. Other state-level reforms included a workmen's compensation law (Maryland, 1902), a ten-hour law for women workers (Oregon, 1903), and a minimum-wage law (Massachusetts, 1912). The National Consumers' League (1899), founded by Hull House resident Florence Kelley, mobilized middle-class support for such measures.

In Wisconsin, Republican congressman Robert La Follette won the governorship in 1900 by challenging his party's domination by railroads and other corporate interests. Working with professors at the University of Wisconsin in Madison, down the street from the capital, La Follette pushed through higher corporate taxes, a state railroad commission, and campaign-spending rules and a direct-primary system to curb corporations' political power.

Progressivism goes national

In September 1901, in Buffalo, New York, an anarchist shot President McKinley. When he died a week later, Vice President Theodore Roosevelt (nicknamed "TR"), the forty-two-year-old former New York governor famed for his exploits in the Spanish-American War, entered the White House. Descended from a prominent Dutch immigrant family, TR believed in a strong presidency to protect the public interest and assure national greatness. He disliked and distrusted the "big money men" who dominated business and politics. Possessing boundless energy and a love of the limelight, Roosevelt revitalized the presidency after years of legislative dominance. As his daughter later observed: "My father always wanted to be the corpse at every funeral, the bride at every wedding, and the baby at every christening."

When coal miners went on strike in 1902, TR reversed his predecessors' antilabor bias and forced the mine owners to accept arbitration granting the miners higher wages and shorter hours.

When J. P. Morgan and other financiers hammered together a trust that controlled railroading in the Northwest, TR's attorney general sued them for violating the Sherman Anti-Trust Act. The Supreme Court upheld the suit, securing Roosevelt's reputation as a "trustbuster." Roosevelt played a key role in passage of the 1906 Hepburn Act granting the Interstate Commerce Commission (ICC) regulatory powers over railroads and outlawing practices by which they curried political and popular favor. (Created in 1887 to regulate railroad abuses, the ICC had been hobbled by hostile court rulings.) That same year, Congress passed the Pure Food and Drug Act and the Meat Inspection Act, regulating unsafe and adulterated foods and medicines, and mandating inspection of the packinghouses graphically described in Sinclair's *The Jungle*.

Recognizing industrialization's toll on nature as well as on society, Roosevelt championed national parks and natural-resource conservation. Protecting millions of acres of public land from unregulated logging and mining, he also backed the National Reclamation Act (1902) designating income from public land sales for dams and irrigation projects.

In 1908, declining to seek a second full term, TR backed Secretary of War William Howard Taft, who won the presidency. Though a more conventional pro-business, high-tariff Republican, Taft did expand federal antitrust prosecutions. Taft alienated tariff reformers and conservationists, however, and in 1912 Roosevelt (back from an African big-game hunting expedition) challenged Taft for the Republican nomination. Failing this, he ran on a third-party ticket, the Progressive Party. (It was nicknamed the "Bull Moose" Party after TR exuberantly proclaimed, "I feel fit as a bull moose.") With the Republicans split, the Democratic candidate, New Jersey governor Woodrow Wilson, a political neophyte and former Princeton University president, won the presidency. The Socialist Eugene Debs garnered 897,000 votes, underscoring the widespread revulsion against uncontrolled capitalist power.

Sustaining the reform spirit, Wilson supported the Underwood Tariff (1913), whose lower rates pleased farmers and consumers. He masterminded Congress's 1913 passage of the Federal Reserve Act, restructuring the nation's banking system under the Federal Reserve Board, a new public-private agency with broad monetary powers. In 1914, again with Wilson's active engagement, Congress created the Federal Trade Commission to regulate unfair competitive practices and passed the Clayton Antitrust Act, strengthening the 1890 Sherman Act by listing specific illegal corporate practices.

In 1916 Wilson backed measures to aid debt-ridden farmers, compensate federal employees for job-related injuries, and ban the products of child labor from interstate commerce. (A conservative Supreme Court ruled this law unconstitutional two years later.) That fall, he won reelection.

Two constitutional amendments, both ratified in 1913, reflected the reform spirit: the Sixteenth, authorizing a federal income tax, and the Seventeenth, providing for the direct election of U.S. senators rather than by state legislatures, where opportunities for corporate influence and bribery abounded. Reform energies continued to bubble up outside Washington as well. The woman's movement, increasingly focused on voting rights, gained strength as younger college-educated and professional women joined the ranks. Under Carrie Chapman Catt, the National American Woman Suffrage Association focused on state suffrage campaigns, including a successful one in California in 1911. Alice Paul's rival organization, emulating British suffragists, concentrated on persuading Congress to enact a woman-suffrage constitutional amendment.

A vanguard of intrepid black leaders and white allies pursued the struggle for racial justice. William Monroe Trotter, editor of the *Boston Guardian*, criticizing Booker T. Washington's public reticence on racial issues, demanded more aggressive challenges.

So, too, did W. E. B. Du Bois, a Harvard-educated historian and professor at Atlanta University (founded by abolitionists in 1865 to educate African Americans) in his pathbreaking work *The Souls of Black Folk* (1903). In 1909 Du Bois and other African Americans, with white supporters, including a grandson of abolitionist William Lloyd Garrison, founded the National Association for the Advancement of Colored People (NAACP). Through its publication, the *Crisis*, edited by DuBois, and a network of local affiliates, the NAACP battled lynching, challenged segregation in the courts, and spearheaded the antiracist campaign.

Progressivism's achievements and blind spots

Progressive reformers mobilized press, pulpit, and politics to address the social problems arising from industrialization, urban growth, and unregulated corporate power. Soon the New Deal (see chap. 7) would draw upon Progressive-era precedents. Decades later, TR's conservationist ethic would inspire the environmental movement.

Yet these early-twentieth-century reformers, mostly white, native-born, and middle class, shared many of their era's prejudices and blind spots. Some blamed immigrants for the problems caused by industrialization; elite Bostonians founded the Immigration Restriction League in 1894, and a 1911 congressional report trumpeted the alleged physical and moral defects of the new immigrants. In *The Passing of the Great Race* (1916), Madison Grant, a prominent environmental conservationist, offered pseudo-scientific data to prove the superiority of the "Nordic" race to Jews, African Americans, and southern and eastern Europeans.

Only a handful of Progressives protested lynching or racial discrimination. Indeed, many southern Progressives *defended* white supremacy and segregation. TR entertained Booker T. Washington at the White House, but otherwise evaded the issue. Woodrow Wilson, a Virginian, praised D. W. Griffith's 1915 film

The Birth of a Nation glorifying the Ku Klux Klan. Under Wilson, segregation pervaded the federal government. As so often in history, the bottom line is mixed: the Progressives' achievements are impressive; their lamentable shortcomings reflective of their time.

Economic imperialism; war in Europe

American capitalists continued to look abroad. In 1899–1900, as European powers pressured China for economic concessions, Secretary of State John Hay issued several so-called Open Door notes asserting U.S. commercial interests in that country. (The term "open door" reflected Washington's interest in open access to Chinese trade.) In 1900 U.S. troops joined an international force that suppressed the Boxer Rebellion, an anti-foreign Chinese uprising. In 1907, demonstrating U.S. sea power, TR sent an armada of U.S. battleships, destroyers, and support vessels on a world tour, including Japan, proud of its own naval might.

TR also worked to assure U.S. access to Latin America as a source of investment opportunities as well as minerals and other commodities. The Boston-based United Fruit Company (founded 1899), importers of bananas, coffee, and other commodities, wielded vast economic and political power in both the United States and Latin America in these years. In what is known as the "Roosevelt Corollary" to the Monroe Doctrine (1904), TR warned that "chronic wrongdoing" by any Latin American nation could bring U.S. military intervention. President Taft, pursuing an approach dubbed "dollar diplomacy," similarly promoted U.S. economic interests abroad.

Underscoring the expansionist dynamic, the United States in 1914 opened the Panama Canal linking the Atlantic and Pacific and promoting world trade. Having acquired a failed French canal-building company in 1902, the Roosevelt administration orchestrated a "revolution" in Panama, then part of Colombia.

With substantial payments to Colombia and newly hatched
Panama, the canal project proceeded.

President Wilson intervened in Mexico, where a 1911 revolution
threatened U.S. oil and mining interests. To overthrow a ruling
general he detested, Wilson in 1914 sent an invading force to Vera
Cruz. In 1916 when a Mexican bandit gang murdered sixteen U.S.
mining engineers and invaded a New Mexico town, Wilson ordered

8. **President Theodore Roosevelt (TR) visits the Panama Canal
construction site in 1906. While the canal symbolized the United
States' emergence as a world power, TR brought an aggressive new
vigor and activism to the presidency.**

150,000 National Guardsmen to the border. As this confrontation unfolded, however, a far graver crisis erupted in Europe.

In June 1914, Austrian Archduke Franz Ferdinand paid a state visit to Bosnia-Herzegovina, recently annexed by Austria. As the archduke and his wife rode through Sarajevo, a young Bosnian Serb, angered by the annexation, shot them dead. Austria promptly declared war on Serbia. Russia joined in on Serbia's side. Other European nations, linked by secret treaties, plunged in as well, with France, Great Britain, and Russia allied on one side, Germany and Austria-Hungary, the so-called Central Powers, on the other. (Italy, initially neutral, joined the Allies in 1915.) The conflict soon degenerated into a grinding stalemate of trench warfare along a front snaking from Belgium to Switzerland. Protracted and inconclusive fighting around Verdun on the Meuse River throughout 1916 took a horrendous toll of more than 300,000 lives.

President Wilson proclaimed U.S. neutrality, and peace advocates won broad support. Neutrality proved difficult, however. Many Americans, especially of the ruling political and financial elite (including Wilson himself), had ancestral and cultural ties to Great Britain and France. Many other Americans had links to Germany and Austria. Irish Americans felt little sympathy for the British cause. Ultimately, the pro-Allied cause proved stronger. As U.S. banks extended loans to the British and French, financial institutions and industrial corporations organized a "preparedness" campaign promoting military rearmament. Fundamentally, America's growing global reach clashed with European imperial ambitions, especially those of the Central Powers.

As in the long-ago War of 1812, the issue of neutral rights became the flashpoint. Both sides menaced U.S. shipping, but German U-boat (submarine) attacks finally propelled America into the war. In May 1915 when a U-boat torpedo sank the British liner *Lusitania* off the Irish coast, the nearly twelve hundred dead included one hundred twenty-eight U.S. citizens. Wilson protested, and for a time Berlin halted such attacks. In January 1917, however, Germany resumed unrestricted submarine warfare. Breaking diplomatic relations, Wilson on April 2 called for a declaration of war. By lopsided margins, the Senate and House approved.

The war in Europe

As an initial war measure, Congress authorized a military draft. Along with 3 million draftees, 1.3 million volunteers and National Guard troops swelled the ranks of service personnel, including 260,000 African Americans and 12,000 Native Americans. The first U.S. troops, called the Allied Expeditionary Force (AEF), reached France in October 1917, just as Bolshevik (communist) revolutionaries seized power in Russia and took Russia out of the war, freeing Germany to shift forces to the Western front.

The AEF commander, General John Pershing, was descended, ironically, from German immigrant ancestors originally named Pfoersching. Appalled by the stalemated trench warfare, Pershing resisted attempts to integrate his troops into French and British units. The Allies set up a unified force under French command early in 1918, but the Americans fought in separate units. AEF troops saw action in March around Amiens on the Somme River in northwestern France, just as Germany launched a major spring offensive. In May, AEF troops helped turn back a German advance south of Amiens. Farther east, along the Marne River, the Germans drove within fifty miles of Paris. Again AEF troops played a key role in halting the advance around Rheims and Chateau-Thierry and a nearby forested area, Belleau Wood.

As an Allied counteroffensive pushed the Germans eastward, the tide turned. More than 250,000 AEF troops fought along the front, from the Somme and the Marne, a salient around St. Mihiel, and finally in the Meuse-Argonne campaign that drove northward through the Argonne forest, taking the vital rail center of Sedan. On November 11, 1918, Germany surrendered.

Such a summary cannot convey the horrors of a war that, by conservative estimates, cost some 10 million military deaths and 7 million civilian deaths, including many from starvation and disease. Russia lost 1.8 million soldiers; France, 1.4 million; Great Britain, 885,000. New killing technologies, including tanks, poison gas, and aerial bombardment, increased the toll. An influenza epidemic that started in the military camps killed at least 50 million persons worldwide.

Given such statistics, America's losses of 49,000 battlefield deaths, plus 63,000 dead of disease, mostly in the influenza epidemic, while large, pale by comparison. Nevertheless, the war affected the nation profoundly, on the home front and in the diplomatic arena no less than on the battlefield.

The war at home

As in earlier conflicts, America's brief engagement in World War I had ramifications far beyond the battlefield. For example, with famine stalking Europe, and Washington feeding a vast army, U.S. farm prices soared. Newly prosperous farmers invested heavily in land and equipment, saddling themselves with debt when prices plummeted after the war.

Washington's economic regulatory role, already expanded in the Progressive era, grew further in 1917–18. One federal agency controlled railroad traffic, giving military requirements top priority. Another, the powerful War Industries Board, headed by the Wall Street investor Bernard Baruch, oversaw industrial production to maximize efficiency. Later, in the Depression-wracked 1930s, President Franklin D. Roosevelt would cite such wartime precedents in calling for governmental intervention to combat the economic crisis.

With war production booming, immigration cut off, and thousands of workers in the military, employers modified long-standing discriminatory hiring practices. Thousands of African Americans migrated from the South seeking jobs in northern factories. While this migration heightened racial tensions in northern cities, the war also exposed black soldiers in France to a less race-obsessed society. All this had profound future implications.

Women, too, seized wartime employment opportunities, taking jobs in factories or in other male-dominated occupations. Returning veterans reclaimed their jobs at war's end, but memories of wartime employment, passed to daughters and granddaughters, helped inspire future campaigns for gender equality in the workplace.

Some Progressive-era reforms gained ground. The War Labor Board, yet another new government agency, supported unionization and improved factory safety and working conditions. As woman-suffrage leaders backed the war effort, support for their cause increased. New York State granted women the vote in November 1917, and the Nineteenth Amendment, extending the franchise to all women, won ratification in 1920. Fueled by wartime moral idealism, the anti-prostitution and anti-alcohol reforms accelerated. (The prominence of German names such as Anheuser-Busch among the big breweries helped the latter cause.) The Eighteenth (Prohibition) Amendment was ratified in 1919. New Orleans closed its red-light district as a war measure, sending jazz musicians northward.

The war affected the home front political and cultural climate. The Wilson administration's propaganda agency, the Committee on Public Information, fanned super-patriotism with posters, parades, and magazine ads. "Four Minute Men" delivered pro-war harangues in movie theaters. Movie stars promoted "Liberty Bond" drives to finance the war. Songwriters offered jaunty pro-war anthems such as George M. Cohan's "Over There." Progressive intellectuals like philosopher John Dewey endorsed the war as an essential step toward a new era of peace and justice abroad and a more activist government role in promoting social justice at home.

As the spirit of unity and idealism turned ugly, however, pacifists, socialists, people with ancestral loyalties to Germany, and other war opponents faced denunciation as traitors. An Illinois jury acquitted the leaders of a mob that hanged a German-American coal miner for criticizing the war. The Boston Symphony Orchestra dismissed its German-American director. Films and posters portrayed German soldiers as sadistic monsters and rapists. The 1918 Espionage Act and the Sedition Amendment (1919) banned socialist and radical publications and criminalized speech critical of the government or the war. Among those arrested and imprisoned was Eugene V. Debs, who remained behind bars until 1921, while garnering over 900,000 votes for president in 1920. As the reactionary mood spread, Republicans captured both houses of Congress in the 1918 midterm election.

Bitter aftermath

Americans greeted the November 1918 armistice with joyous demonstrations, but the war's consequences proved far different from what President Wilson and the nation hoped for. American troops joined an international force aimed at overthrowing Russia's new communist regime, an irritant contributing to future hostility. Wilson attended the 1919 peace conference at Versailles (becoming the first president to travel abroad while in office), but the results mostly dismayed him. France, Great Britain, and Italy imposed vindictive peace terms, demanded punitive reparation payments, and sliced off tracts of German and Austrian territory, spawning festering resentments in the defeated nations.

Wilson's one great achievement at Versailles was to incorporate into the treaty a pledge, or "covenant," by the Allies to form a new international peacekeeping organization, the League of Nations. But in October 1919, while on a grueling national tour to promote

Senate ratification of the treaty, Wilson collapsed. Rushed back to Washington, he suffered a devastating stroke that left him a querulous invalid, out of touch with political reality. Wilson's illness and the isolationist political shift combined to doom the treaty, despite some senators' efforts to forge a compromise over the controversial League of Nations covenant. In a November 1919 vote in which senators bitterly opposed to the League, led by Henry Cabot Lodge of Massachusetts, joined with fervent league supporters following Wilson's instructions to refuse any compromise, the Senate finally rejected the treaty. The United States would not enter the League of Nations. Wilson's final years—he died in 1924—were sad and embittered, as one of the more remarkable political careers in U.S. history ended in failure and frustration. Wilson would not live to see the United States join the league's successor, the United Nations, in 1945.

Domestically, the reactionary climate already in evidence during the war intensified. White hostility to southern blacks seeking new opportunities in the North hardened. The number of lynchings surged, including some of black veterans still in uniform. In 1919 anti-black riots hit Omaha, Chicago, and other cities. As the anti-radical hysteria deepened, the House of Representatives refused to seat a Milwaukee socialist, Victor Berger. The mayor of Seattle called in federal troops to suppress a general strike. In January 1920 a Justice Department anti-radical division under the young J. Edgar Hoover (future head of the Federal Bureau of Investigation) arrested several thousand suspected radicals in a coordinated series of "Red Raids." Hundreds were imprisoned and aliens deported with minimal legal process.

The war that America had entered with such high idealism in April 1917 had dragged to its end in a climate of reaction and isolationism that would persist in the decade ahead. Neither domestically nor internationally did the war achieve what its supporters had hoped. The Progressive movement of a few years earlier seemed a dim memory as the nation moved uneasily into the 1920s.

Chapter 7

1920–1945: From conflict to global power

The quarter century from 1920 to 1945 transformed America. In 1920 the United States, while an industrial powerhouse, remained a provincial society on the margins of global affairs. By 1945, in a war-shattered world, its domestic politics reshaped by the New Deal of the 1930s, America stood preeminent. In these same years, intellectuals, social thinkers, and cultural creators challenged their predecessors' moral certitudes to forge a modern, cosmopolitan society.

The 1920s: political reaction, social tensions, cultural ferment

The Roaring Twenties once enjoyed mythic status in American memory. Reinforced by popular histories such as Frederick Lewis Allen's *Only Yesterday* (1930), this mythology evoked an exuberant, hedonistic decade when Americans, abandoning traditional taboos and Wilsonian idealism, flocked to jazz clubs and patronized Prohibition-era speakeasies supplied with liquor by colorful gangsters like Chicago's Al Capone.

The Roaring Twenties image captures part of the decade's reality. For some affluent college students, chronicled in F. Scott Fitzgerald's 1920 novel *This Side of Paradise*, the 1920s did, indeed, bring a heady sense of escape from old restraints. As automobile ownership mushroomed thanks to Henry Ford's mass-production feats, millions of Americans enjoyed new mobility. Motor vehicle registrations, under 2 million in 1914, approached 27 million by 1930. The spread of radio, Hollywood movies, recorded music, and national advertising spawned a new mass culture. Sports heroes like baseball's Babe Ruth and boxing's Jack Dempsey basked in the media spotlight. When the daredevil pilot Charles Lindbergh flew nonstop from New York to Paris in 1927, a celebrity-obsessed nation erupted in a celebratory frenzy.

Beyond the surface froth and the chug-chug of Ford cars lie more complex realities. Politically, the postwar conservative reaction continued. The 1920 Republican presidential candidate, Ohio senator Warren G. Harding, won in a landslide. Apart from a

9. Maude Younger works on her Ford car in Washington, DC, having driven from San Francisco to attend the 1920 conference of the National Woman's Party, of which she was legislative secretary. Even as American women won the right to vote, the advent of the automobile gave them a liberating sense of freedom and mobility.

1922 Washington conference where the world's naval powers agreed to limit warship construction, Harding's scandal-ridden presidency accomplished little. Harding succumbed to a bad heart in 1923, succeeded by his vice president, Calvin Coolidge. A taciturn Vermonter, Coolidge differed superficially from the convivial Harding. Shrewd public relations—an emerging profession in the 1920s—enhanced his image as a Yankee of granite-like integrity. But the Coolidge administration, while more honest, differed little in its conservative, corporate orientation, summed up in Coolidge's laconic aphorism. "The business of America is business."

When Coolidge declined to run in 1928, Commerce Secretary Herbert Hoover won the Republican nomination and the presidency, defeating New York governor Al Smith, a Catholic of immigrant origins. General prosperity and anti-Catholic prejudice helped Hoover at the ballot box, but the immigrant cities went Democratic, signaling changes ahead. A self-made mining engineer of Quaker upbringing, Hoover as a wartime food administrator and then as commerce secretary had espoused governmental activism, more in the spirit of Theodore Roosevelt than Harding or Coolidge. When floods devastated the Mississippi Valley in 1927, he had rushed to the region to coordinate private relief efforts. As president, he initiated research on public-policy issues and assembled corporate leaders to discuss greater efficiencies through voluntary cooperation. Despite promising beginnings, however, a stock market crash and its consequences overwhelmed Hoover's presidency and shattered his reputation.

American society in the 1920s exhibited severe stresses as citizens grappled with technological change, ideological turmoil, and social strains arising from urbanization, immigration, and African Americans' northward migration. Underscoring the urban shift, the 1920 census found for the first time most Americans living in towns and cities.

The decade saw a resurgence of the Ku Klux Klan, the Reconstruction-era white supremacist movement. Thanks to shrewd marketing, Klan membership in the early 1920s spread beyond the South into the Midwest and Far West. White-robed Protestant KKK members marched, rallied, and burned crosses in the night to intimidate blacks, Catholics, and those suspected of loose morals. The national movement soon collapsed amid a sordid sex scandal involving the head of the Indiana Klan, but its intolerant and intimidating message persisted.

Many working-class African Americans rallied to Marcus Garvey, a charismatic Jamaican. With parades and uniforms, members of Garvey's Universal Negro Improvement Association (UNIA) championed his message of black pride, race-based enterprises, and an eventual return to Mother Africa. The movement alarmed white America as well as the NAACP, with its goal of racial integration. Garvey's 1927 mail-fraud conviction and subsequent deportation weakened the UNIA, but it remains a noteworthy early instance of mass mobilization among African Americans.

When two Italian immigrant anarchists, Nicola Sacco and Bartolomeo Vanzetti, were convicted and sentenced to death for the 1920 murder of a paymaster and guard in a South Braintree, Massachusetts, factory robbery, their defenders saw anti-radical, anti-immigrant prejudice at work. Despite widespread protests, a commission of notables upheld the verdict, and in 1927 the two were electrocuted. "All right, we are two nations," concluded an anguished prose poem by the young writer John Dos Passos. Later findings tended to confirm the verdicts, but the Sacco-Vanzetti case still symbolizes the nation's bitter divisions in the 1920s.

Although liberal religious leaders had long accepted Darwin's theory of evolution, Protestant fundamentalists, already upset by critical biblical scholarship, theological "Modernism," and the rise of a secular cosmopolitan culture, rejected Darwinism as a threat to their belief in biblical inerrancy. When Tennessee outlawed the teaching of evolution in public schools, a teacher in Dayton, Tennessee, John Scopes, challenged the law, supported by the American Civil Liberties Union and by local merchants hoping to drum up business. Scopes's 1925 trial drew national attention, with celebrity participants including the iconoclastic journalist Henry L. Mencken, defense lawyer Clarence Darrow, and William Jennings Bryan testifying for the prosecution. The Scopes trial and its inconclusive outcome hardly destroyed fundamentalism, as some claimed, but it further underscored the decade's deep cultural fissures.

The twenties also brought a burst of cultural creativity, as young writers and playwrights, some living as expatriates in Paris, produced work of startling freshness and originality. In *A Farewell to Arms*, Ernest Hemingway dismissed the idealistic rhetoric of 1917–18 and portrayed the reality of mass slaughter. Sinclair Lewis in *Main Street* and *Babbitt* satirized American middle-class provincialism and anti-intellectualism. F. Scott Fitzgerald's *The Great Gatsby* probed the superficiality and heedless arrogance of postwar America's privileged elite. Talented black writers, artists, and musicians produced work of innovative artistry in the Harlem Renaissance. Louis Armstrong, Fletcher Henderson, Edward ("Duke") Ellington, and other jazz greats brought this uniquely American musical genre, with its African roots, to a broad public. Across the cultural landscape, creative ferment and modernist challenges to the old order, along with notable achievements in science, made this one of the more intellectually productive epochs in U.S. history, belying stereotypes of giddy mindlessness and philistine conventionality.

Depression and reform

The 1920s exuded a glow of prosperity, buoyed by incessant advertising and consumer demand for automobiles, radios, and electric appliances. Housing construction boomed. Families took vacations and flocked to movies and sports events. Prosperity had limits, though. Debt-ridden farmers suffered as commodity prices tumbled from war-time peaks. Immigrant working-class families struggled to make ends meet. In a racist age, most African Americans and Native Americans lived on the economic margins.

As the decade progressed, warning signals mounted. Lagging consumer income produced a glut of housing, automobiles, and consumer goods. The construction industry faltered; factory inventories crept up. Stock prices soared as speculators and novices, many buying on credit, drove prices ever higher. The crash came in October 1929, as the stock market collapsed and paper fortunes evaporated. Belying President Hoover's optimistic pronouncements, a long-term depression set in as unemployment rose, production fell, banks failed, and fear stalked the land. A global deflationary spiral in 1931 worsened the crisis. By 1933, 25 percent of American workers were jobless, with millions more underemployed. True to his voluntarist ideology, Hoover urged private organizations to redouble relief efforts. In 1932, however, he did support Congress's creation of a new agency, the Reconstruction Finance Corporation (RFC), to extend credit to banks and other financial institutions to pump capital into the economy and even make loans to state and local relief programs.

The Great Depression deepened, however, and in 1932 voters repudiated Hoover and resoundingly elected New York's Democratic governor, Franklin D. Roosevelt (FDR), as president, along with a Democratic Congress. Of an old patrician family, he was distantly related to Theodore Roosevelt. A 1921 polio attack left him unable to walk but toughened his spirit and deepened his empathy for human suffering. Roosevelt's campaign speeches offered few specifics, though he did promise a "new deal," unwittingly naming an era. In contrast to Hoover, FDR exuded confidence, optimism, and receptivity to experimentation. He recruited young administrators and advisors (including Jews and Catholics, hitherto excluded from Washington's inner circles) who shared his innovative proclivities.

Taking office on a wave of goodwill, Roosevelt first addressed immediate crises. To restore confidence in the banks he backed legislation insuring deposits and tightening bank regulations. Addressing the employment crisis, Congress at FDR's initiative appropriated emergency relief funds, set up the Public Works Administration (PWA) to hire workers on infrastructure projects, and created the Civilian Conservation Corps (CCC) that put jobless youth to work on reforestation, trail maintenance, and other projects in parks and wilderness areas. The New Deal's most innovative early program, the TVA (Tennessee Valley Authority), built dams and hydroelectric power plants in the Tennessee River basin, providing electricity, erosion-and-flood control, and recreational facilities for an impoverished region.

Two early New Deal programs promoted long-term recovery. The Agricultural Adjustment Administration (AAA) aimed to raise farm prices by paying farmers to cut production of basic commodities. The National Recovery Administration (NRA), echoing Hoover's theme of business-government cooperation, proposed to stimulate industrial recovery and forestall deflation through voluntary codes negotiated by corporate leaders pledging to maintain employment and uphold prices and wages. Cooperating industries displayed a "We Do Our Part" poster. The NRA reflected FDR's early goal of rallying all sectors of society, including business, to his recovery program. Problems plagued these agencies, however. The NRA staggered under bureaucratic complexity; the AAA raised overall farm income, but farm laborers, sharecroppers, and migrant workers benefitted little. Few mourned when the Supreme Court declared these programs unconstitutional in 1935.

Facing Republican opposition and challengers on the left, including Louisiana's demagogic governor Huey Long, FDR shifted course in 1934–35. Downplaying the national-unity theme, he embraced more partisan, class-based legislation, regulatory measures, and tax policies. At FDR's initiative, Congress raised taxes on corporations and the richest Americans; set up the Works Progress Administration (WPA) to create public jobs more quickly than the slow-moving PWA; and created the Securities and Exchange Commission to more closely regulate the stock market. The New Deal's two most lasting measures also date to 1935. The National Labor Relations Act, reversing decades of government hostility to organized labor, guaranteed unions' collective bargaining rights and outlawed various anti-union tactics. A surge of unionization in the automobile, steel, and other industries soon followed. Of equal long-term significance, the Social Security Act created a federal-state program of old age pensions, unemployment benefits, and aid to families with dependent children. Though excluding farmers and the self-employed, this law established a national welfare system that would be extended—and debated—in future years, reshaping the American social contract.

Underscoring the New Deal's leftward shift, Roosevelt in the 1936 campaign denounced "the malefactors of great wealth" and welcomed their opposition. Winning by a landslide, FDR soon proposed a plan to enlarge the nine-member Supreme Court. Dominated by conservatives, the high court had struck down several New Deal measures, and Roosevelt feared the reform measures of 1935 would meet the same fate. His "court packing" scheme failed, underscoring the restraints limiting even this most popular president, but as several older justices retired, FDR replaced them with judges more sympathetic to the New Deal. A sharp recession in 1937–38, triggered by relief-spending cuts and Social Security payroll deductions, again pushed up unemployment and helped produce Republican gains in the 1938 midterm election. Roosevelt responded with a new round of stimulus measures, but unemployment in 1940 still stood at 14.6 percent. By that year, when FDR won an unprecedented third term, ominous developments abroad overshadowed home-front issues.

Reliant on the votes of southern white Democratic legislators, Roosevelt sidestepped racial issues, including NAACP pleas to make lynching a federal crime. The administration did support symbolic measures, including a 1939 concert at the Lincoln Memorial by the black contralto Marian Anderson, after the Daughters of the American Revolution barred her from performing in their Washington auditorium. FDR's politically active wife, Eleanor, deeply engaged with social-justice issues, deplored racial discrimination and prodded her husband on this and other causes.

The New Deal's depression-fighting record was mixed. Some early programs proved ineffective. Relief and public-works programs helped the jobless in the short run, but only World War II restored full employment. FDR, a budgetary conservative, rejected deficit spending as an economic stimulus, as advocated by the British economist John Maynard Keynes. Since government bonds financed New Deal spending, the stimulus effect was minimal.

Still, the New Deal remains a watershed in American history. Alphabet-soup agencies such as the CCC, WPA, and TVA strengthened the nation's public-works infrastructure and national parks. WPA cultural programs supported artists, dramatists, musicians, and writers. The more radical measures of 1934–35 encouraged unionization, toughened financial regulation, moderated class disparities through progressive tax policies, and created the rudiments of a social safety net. Despite conservatives' criticism, FDR was a reformer, not a revolutionary. He sought to save capitalism by moderating its abuses, not destroy it. Praised, demonized, and emulated, the New Deal remains a basic point of reference across the ideological spectrum. Just as the New Deal reshaped U.S. political culture, World War II would profoundly enlarge America's global role.

War and global power

Few Americans in 1930 foresaw an imminent plunge into another war. In fact, the post-1918 reaction against Wilsonian internationalism fed a determination—deeply rooted in

American history—to avoid foreign entanglements. Muckraking exposés of the bankers and industrialists who had pushed for war in 1917 intensified this reaction. By the mid-1930s a peace movement swept college campuses, and Congress passed a series of neutrality acts to prevent U.S. involvement in future conflicts.

Worsening world conditions mocked such hopes. Italian fascists under Benito Mussolini seized power as early as 1922. In 1937, as an expansionist, militaristic Japan invaded China, Japanese troops unleashed an orgy of killing and rape in Nanking (now Nanjing). In Germany, Adolf Hitler's National Socialist (Nazi) Party gained power in 1933, intimidating domestic opponents and pursing its agenda of ridding Germany of Jews, socialists, and communists; avenging the punitive Versailles Treaty; and seeking *Lebensraum* (living space) beyond Germany's eastern borders. Foreshadowing the conflict ahead, the Spanish Civil War (1936–39) pitted General Francisco Franco's fascist army against supporters of Spain's elected republican government. While Hitler supported Franco, Russia backed the communists in the Republican coalition. Some U.S. volunteers, organized as the Abraham Lincoln Brigade, fought with the Republican forces before Franco crushed them.

In 1939 Hitler and the Russian dictator Josef Stalin concluded a non-aggression treaty including secret clauses splitting Poland between them. This cynical pact disillusioned American supporters of the so-called Popular Front, a Moscow-backed alliance of communists and non-communists in opposition to fascism. When Germany invaded Poland on September 1, 1939, England and France declared war. In spring 1940, Germany occupied Norway, Denmark, the Netherlands, and Belgium, and invaded France. In June, as British troops withdrew from Dunkirk across the English Channel, France surrendered. As Nazi warplanes bombed English cities, England's prime minister Winston Churchill pled for U.S. support.

Though convinced that America must ultimately fight, FDR proceeded cautiously. As an "America First" movement rallied isolationist sentiment, Roosevelt in 1937 called vaguely for a "quarantine" of aggressive nations. When Europe went to war in September 1939, FDR reaffirmed U.S. neutrality but added that he could not (as Wilson had) ask Americans to remain neutral in thought. In 1940 Congress authorized an arms build-up and the first peacetime draft. Under the Lend-Lease Act (March 1941), Congress approved $7 billion in credits to help cash-strapped Britain buy U.S. armaments. With FDR's approval, U.S. convoys protected the ships transporting the armaments across the Atlantic.

By June 1941 German armies had invaded Russia and by November reached the outskirts of Moscow. For the United States, all ambiguity ended on December 7, 1941, when Japanese warplanes attacked the U.S. fleet at Pearl Harbor in Hawaii, sinking or disabling nineteen U.S. warships and 150 planes, and killing 2,335 U.S. servicemen. The next day, Congress declared war on the Axis powers—Japan, Germany, and Italy. Volunteers and draftees poured into training camps, factories converted to military production, and Americans rallied behind the war. At several wartime meetings, Roosevelt and Churchill cemented a "Grand Alliance" to coordinate overall strategy and war aims.

In the European war, after defeating General Erwin Rommel's German forces in North Africa, Allied troops early in 1943 invaded Sicily and then Italy, fighting their way northward. Italy left the war in July, and by summer 1944 Germany's remaining troops in Italy had withdrawn. On June 6, 1944—D-Day—160,000 Allied troops under U.S. general Dwight Eisenhower waded ashore on France's Normandy coast, in the largest amphibious operation in history. Despite fierce German resistance, they pushed across France, liberated Paris in August, and by early 1945 advanced into Germany itself. American and British bombers blasted German industrial sites and in raids of increasing ferocity hit Berlin,

10. **Prime Minister Winston Churchill and President Franklin D. Roosevelt meet at Casablanca, Morocco, in January 1943. Proclaiming "unconditional surrender" as the Allied war aim, they also debated the location of a second front against Nazi Germany. In several wartime meetings the two leaders built a close working relationship.**

Hamburg, and other cities. A devastating February 1945 raid destroyed the ancient and beautiful city of Dresden on the Danube, killing more than twenty-five thousand. Beginning in 1944, German V-1 and V-2 rockets rained down on London, Antwerp, and other cities. The era of "total war," including the deliberate targeting of civilians, had arrived.

On the Eastern Front, meanwhile, Russian troops broke the terrible German sieges of Stalingrad and Leningrad and drove back the invaders. Grinding across Eastern Europe, the Russians by April 1945 crossed into Germany. As Russians approached from the east and British, American, and other Allied forces from the west, the pincers closed. A December 1944 German counteroffensive, the Battle of the Bulge, failed. As the Russians reached Berlin, Hitler and his mistress committed suicide in his underground bunker. On May 7, 1945, Germany surrendered. President Roosevelt did not live to see the day. He died of a cerebral hemorrhage on April 12, and was succeeded by his vice president, Harry Truman.

Meanwhile, in the Pacific, Japan made significant gains after Pearl Harbor, attacking various strongholds of Western colonial power. The Philippines, still held by the United States, fell early in 1942. Reports of Japanese atrocities, including the "Bataan Death March" of U.S. prisoners captured in the Philippines, intensified hatred of the Asian foe. Reversing the tide, a U.S. island-hopping campaign moved inexorably toward Japan. Having secured Guadalcanal in the Solomon Islands in February 1943, G.I.s took fiercely defended Japanese strongholds in the Gilbert, Marshall, and Mariana island groups. By February 1945 the Philippines had been retaken. After Iwo Jima in the Marianas fell in March 1945, a photograph of G.I.s raising the flag on Mount Suribachi became an iconic image of the war. Okinawa, the last Japanese stronghold before the home islands, surrendered in June. The U.S. also prevailed in a series of naval engagements—including the Coral Sea and Midway battles (1942) and Leyte Gulf (October 1944). From hastily built island airfields, U.S. bombers pounded Japanese cities. A March 1945 raid on Tokyo by 375 B-29 bombers unleashed a firestorm that killed an estimate 100,000 men, women, and children.

On August 6 and August 9, 1945, two U.S. atomic bombs destroyed Hiroshima and Nagasaki, killing many thousands in the initial blast and fire, and thousands more from radiation exposure. The atomic bomb, based on theoretical work by European physicists, some of whom had emigrated to America as refugees from Nazism, was the product of a secret wartime undertaking, code named the Manhattan Project, funded by President Roosevelt in 1942. The bombs' components were assembled at facilities in

Hanford, Washington; Oak Ridge, Tennessee; the University of Chicago; and Los Alamos, New Mexico. After a successful July 1945 test in New Mexico, President Truman (attending a postwar conference of the Allied leaders at Potsdam outside Berlin) authorized using the new weapon against Japan. The Hiroshima bomb was dropped on August 6. Two days later, fulfilling a pledge by Stalin at the wartime Yalta conference, the Soviet Union declared war on Japan. Five days after the Nagasaki bomb, Japan surrendered. Thanks to nuclear physics and the Manhattan Project, the mass slaughter of civilian populations, already a feature of the air war, could now be accomplished instantly, by a single bomb.

Were the atomic bombings justified? Many historians believe that Japan would certainly have surrendered before the planned invasion late in 1945, even without the atomic bomb, particularly had the Allies agreed (as they eventually did) to let Emperor Hirohito remain. Others see the timing of the Hiroshima bombing, hours before Russia's promised war declaration, as linked to Washington's postwar strategic calculations involving U.S.-Soviet relations. Whatever the answers, most Americans endorsed President Truman's triumphant claim: the atomic bomb had won the war and saved American lives. As in 1918, delirious crowds again celebrated victory.

Aftermath

World War II left more than 400,000 Americans dead and 672,000 wounded. As in World War I, even this toll pales in comparison to the physical destruction and seventeen million military and twenty million civilian deaths worldwide, including millions of Jews and others who perished in Nazi death camps. But given Japan's surprise attack and imperial ambitions, and Germany's genocidal ideology, most have judged the war justified. In later years, after Vietnam and other controversial military interventions, Americans would recall World War II as "the good war," and the dwindling ranks of veterans who fought in it as "the greatest generation."

As always, the war had social, economic, and cultural ramifications. Large numbers of Americans found jobs in war plants, accelerating long-term urbanization trends. As in 1917–18, many thousands of African Americans and women entered the labor force. War mobilization ended the Depression and led to a postwar economic boom as factories turned to peacetime production, launching an era of consumer abundance—at least for the white middle class. Mass-produced housing for war workers provided a template for postwar suburban housing developments. The 1944 Servicemen's Readjustment Act, dubbed the "G.I. Bill," granted veterans tuition assistance, boosting enrollments in colleges, universities, and technical schools. War propaganda again unleashed ugly passions. Anti-Japanese propaganda in comic books, newspaper cartoons, and Hollywood films employed vicious ethnic stereotypes. In 1942 some 120,000 West Coast Japanese-Americans were uprooted and imprisoned in remote camps—an action supported by the Roosevelt administration and upheld by the U.S. Supreme Court.

Wartime technological innovations profoundly shaped the postwar world. German advances in rocketry foreshadowed the intercontinental ballistic missiles of the Cold War era. Indeed, a leader of the Nazis' rocket program, Wernher von Braun, would play a key role in developing American ICBMs. Wartime computer research laid the groundwork for the postwar computer revolution. The atomic bomb introduced an era of doomsday weaponry that still hangs over the world.

The war shifted the tectonic plates of global power, with profound implications for America's future. With Germany and Japan devastated, Europe prostrate, and Russia hemorrhaging from massive losses, the United States, physically unscathed, stood supreme as the world's superpower, seemingly fulfilling Henry Luce's 1941 *Life* magazine editorial proclaiming "the American Century."

In 1945, delegates from fifty countries gathered in San Francisco to launch the United Nations, modeled on the League of Nations. Like Woodrow Wilson in 1919, many fervently hoped the UN would finally banish war through negotiation and collective action. Yet even as the UN took shape, a dangerous new confrontation loomed. Henry Luce's proud hegemonic boast did not go unchallenged. The Soviet Union, America's wartime ally, soon emerged as a rival for global influence. From the rubble of World War II arose a new conflict, the Cold War.

Chapter 8
1945–1968: Affluence and social unrest

Early postwar America presents a strangely mixed picture of material abundance and mass-culture distractions amid Cold War alarms and a menacing nuclear arms race. Even on the home front, anti-communist paranoia and festering inequities of race, gender, and social class roiled the deceptively bland surface of 1950s America. By the 1960s, revived activist energies produced a surge of reform legislation, civil-rights protests, and anti–Vietnam War demonstrations. As unrest crested in 1968, a sharp political backlash signaled a major conservative shift in U.S. life and culture.

Cold War confrontations

Even during World War II, the "Big Three" alliance of the United States, Great Britain, and the Soviet Union had been beset by tensions, as Stalin pushed his partners to open a Second Front. With the war's end, the alliance quickly fragmented. As British imperial might faded, the United States, with global strategic and corporate interests, confronted a hostile Soviet Union. Stalin, pathologically fearful of future German threats, imposed pro-Soviet regimes on Poland and East Germany. In Western Europe, Italian and French communist parties demonstrated alarming strength. In a belligerent February 1946 speech, Stalin denounced "Western imperialism." That March, in President

Truman's home state of Missouri, Winston Churchill responded. The Soviets had lowered an "iron curtain" across Europe, he declared, and must be resisted. The Cold War had begun.

At the UN, Russia rejected an American plan for international atomic-energy control, charging (with justification) that it would perpetuate U.S. atomic supremacy. In Iran, under joint Allied control during the war, Russia withdrew its troops only in May 1946, under U.S. pressure. (American and British companies promptly negotiated agreements to import Iranian oil.) In Greece, a communist-led insurgency battled the country's reactionary monarchy. In a March 1947 address to Congress proposing aid to Greece, President Truman, heeding a Republican senator's advice that to win bipartisan support he must "scare hell out of the American people," cast the Greek civil war, as well as political instability in nearby Turkey, as part of an apocalyptic global struggle between freedom and tyranny. That June, Secretary of State George Marshall proposed a massive aid program to devastated Europe. While promoting European recovery, Marshall Plan aid reduced the prospects of communist advances; funneled billions to U.S. corporations producing equipment for export; and promoted multination economic cooperation, laying the groundwork for the future European Union.

The diplomat George Kennan's "Containment" doctrine, outlined in a July 1947 *Foreign Affairs* article, "The Sources of Soviet Conduct," provided the early Cold War's ideological framework. (The article was signed simply "X," but Kennan was widely known as the author.)

As Moscow probed for weak spots on Russia's periphery, Kennan argued, the West must vigilantly "contain" the Soviets within their existing sphere of influence. Other administration officials and Washington policymakers vastly expanded Kennan's essentially defensive and cautious strategic vision. Embracing an increasingly alarmist view of the communist threat, they urged a massive military buildup, including nuclear weapons.

In February 1948 a pro-Soviet coup led by Klement Gottwald seized power in Czechoslovakia. That June, as Washington prepared to recognize a separate West German government, Russian authorities blocked land access to Berlin, deep inside East Germany. Rather than risk war by challenging the blockade, U.S. authorities organized a massive airlift to supply Berliners' needs. In May 1949 Russia lifted the blockade. With U.S. backing, the German Federal Republic was created and integrated into the North Atlantic Treaty Organization (NATO), a U.S.-led military alliance. In East Germany, Moscow set up the communist-ruled German Democratic Republic. Churchill's Iron Curtain seemed destined for a very long life. In 1949, as Chinese communists under Mao Zedong defeated Chiang Kai-shek's U.S.-backed regime, the resulting Sino-Soviet alliance intensified fears of communism's seeming inexorable advance.

When the Soviet Union tested an atomic bomb in September 1949, President Truman authorized development of the vastly more powerful hydrogen bomb. Amid deepening fears of global thermonuclear war, a doom-laden 1950 National Security Council document, NSC-68, cast the Cold War in quasi-religious terms, portraying America in a death struggle with Russia, "animated by a new fanatic faith" and bent on "world domination." Reducing the complexity of world affairs to this single apocalyptic confrontation, NSC-68 saw little scope for diplomacy and offered no ideas for moderating the risks, only an "indefinite period of tension and danger." Nothing but a massive military buildup could save the American people who "in the ascendancy of their strength stand in their deepest peril." NSC-68, a major ideological escalation of the Cold War, presented it as a zero-sum game in which one side must win, the other lose. It offered a wholly militarized vision of America's world mission earlier articulated by Woodrow Wilson and, long before that, by the New England Puritans.

Actual conflict erupted not in Europe, as many anticipated, but in distant Korea. When Japan's occupation of Korea ended in 1945,

Russia and the United States demarcated their respective spheres of influence at the 38th parallel. On July 25, 1950, with Moscow's approval, North Korean troops swept across this boundary and drove southward. The UN Security Council, taking advantage of a Soviet boycott, authorized a military response. In September, an amphibious landing at Inchon planned by General Douglas MacArthur, commander of the UN forces, pushed the invaders back across the 38th parallel and advanced into North Korea. By November, as MacArthur's forces approached the Chinese border, Chinese troops entered the war in massive numbers. MacArthur, intent on overthrowing China's communist regime, criticized Truman's orders in letters to sympathetic congressmen. Dismissed by Truman for insubordination in April 1951, MacArthur came home to a hero's welcome.

Armistice talks soon began, but fighting continued until 1953. Sometimes called "the forgotten war," sandwiched between World War II and Vietnam, the Korean War nevertheless cost the lives of 36,516 American soldiers in combat and from other causes, plus some three thousand dead among other UN forces and a vastly higher toll of Chinese dead and Korean casualties, military and civilian. Sixty years later, Korea remained divided between a thriving, Western-oriented South and an impoverished, isolated (and nuclear-armed) North.

The war hero Dwight Eisenhower won the 1952 Republican presidential nomination and the election, and Washington's Cold War preoccupations widened. Eisenhower's secretary of state John Foster Dulles negotiated anti-communist military alliances in Asia and the Middle East. Coups planned by the Central Intelligence Agency (established in 1947) overthrew anti-U.S. or left-leaning regimes in Iran (1953) and Guatemala (1954); U.S. propaganda agencies fomented resistance behind the Iron Curtain. When Soviet tanks crushed an uprising in Hungary in 1956, however, the U.S. did nothing. Even Middle Eastern policy reflected contradictory aims, as Washington simultaneously sought to counter Soviet influence, protect its Persian Gulf oil sources, and support Israel, a Jewish state established in 1948 over Palestinian and Arab opposition.

After Stalin's death in 1953, his successor Nikita Khrushchev moderated Soviet policy and even denounced Stalin's dictatorship. The nuclear weapons and missile competition raged on, however. In October 1957 Soviet scientists launched a space satellite, *Sputnik*, triggering panicky U.S. efforts to toughen math and science instruction.

In 1958, responding to grassroots anti-nuclear pressures in the United States and elsewhere, Washington and Moscow temporarily halted atmospheric testing. The brief Cold War thaw continued in 1959 as Vice President Richard Nixon visited Russia and Khrushchev toured the United States. But a scheduled 1960 Paris summit conference between Eisenhower and Khrushchev, already clouded by events in Cuba, collapsed when the Soviets shot down a U.S. spy plane over Russia.

In 1960 Richard Nixon narrowly lost the presidential race to a charismatic young Massachusetts Democratic senator, John F. Kennedy, who thereby became the first Roman Catholic to win the presidency, another landmark in a society long disfigured by anti-Catholic prejudice. Kennedy's early initiatives included the popular Peace Corps, which recruited young Americans for two years of voluntary service in developing countries. Otherwise, however, his administration got off to a rocky start internationally. At a 1961 Vienna summit, Khrushchev, judging Kennedy weak and inexperienced, threatened to again blockade Berlin. In a grim TV speech, Kennedy warned of nuclear war and announced accelerated civil-defense preparations.

Meanwhile, a new Cold War front opened in Cuba. Insurgents under Fidel Castro overthrew Cuba's pro-U.S. strongman Fulgencio Batista in 1959 and soon allied Cuba with Moscow.

A 1961 invasion of Cuba by CIA-trained exiles aimed at overthrowing Castro, approved by Kennedy though originally authorized by Eisenhower, failed disastrously. Emboldened, the Soviets installed nuclear missiles in Cuba targeting the eastern United States. When U.S. intelligence discovered these missiles in October 1962, Kennedy demanded their removal and challenged Russian ships en route to Cuba. After tense days when nuclear war loomed ominously, Khrushchev backed down. In return for a U.S. pledge not to invade Cuba (and a secret agreement negotiated by the president's brother, Attorney General Robert Kennedy, to remove U.S. missiles from Turkey), Khrushchev withdrew the Cuban missiles. Chastened, the two sides pursued diplomacy. In 1963, as the U.S. anti-nuclear movement gained momentum, they concluded a Limited Nuclear Test Ban Treaty, permanently halting atmospheric nuclear tests, and scheduled further arms-limitation negotiations.

Home-front America in the fifties: affluence and anxiety

On the domestic front, with the avuncular Dwight Eisenhower in the White House, all seemed superficially well in 1950s America, as a cornucopia of consumer goods poured from the nation's factories. Credit cards, introduced in 1950, facilitated the boom. American capitalism, declared one economist, had "left every other system in recorded history far behind." After fifteen years of Depression and war, Americans pursued the good life. For many, the dream seemed attainable. Middle-class and many working-class white families flocked to burgeoning suburbs. A postwar baby boom boosted the sizzling economy. Leisure pursuits proliferated. California's Disneyland opened in 1955. The interstate highway system (launched in 1956) facilitated vacation travel, as did motel chains and fast-food franchises. Foreseeing a rosy future, *Life* magazine declared in 1954: "Looking ahead 10 years, 25 years, there is nothing to hold us back."

While radio and mass magazines remained popular, the newest medium, television, swept the nation; fifty million households owned TV sets by 1960. Comedy series such as *I Love Lucy* and Westerns such as *Gunsmoke* attracted millions of viewers; TV advertisers hawked cars and refrigerators, shampoos and shaving cream. Such programs as *Father Knows Best* and *Leave It to Beaver* offered rose-tinted images of suburban togetherness, with kindly dads, happy housewife moms, and cheerful kids.

Church membership soared as newcomers to suburbia sought friendship and social ties. While thousands flocked to Billy Graham's revivals, others found solace in the positive-thinking books of Norman Vincent Peale. Reflecting the prevailing piety while highlighting America's contrast with the officially atheistic Soviet Union, Congress added "under God" to the pledge of allegiance and "In God We Trust" to the nation's currency.

Beneath the surface, however, lurked problems. Amid abundance, millions lived in poverty. A stark black-white income differential reflected the ugly reality of racial discrimination. Growing numbers of Hispanic immigrants, including migrant farm laborers and domestic workers, struggled on the margins. Despite TV's celebration of domesticity, 40 percent of American women worked, most from economic necessity.

Movies like *The Wild One* (1953), *Blackboard Jungle* (1955), and *Rebel without a Cause* (1955) portrayed marauding motorcycle gangs, turbulent inner-city schools, and rebellious middle-class youth. In literature Allen Ginsberg's *Howl* (1955), Jack Kerouac's *On the Road* (1957), and other works of the so-called Beat movement offered unsettling visions of alienated loners in a conformist, anxiety-ridden society. In the popular-music realm, crooners like Bing Crosby and Perry Como gave way to rock 'n' roll, especially the raw, erotically charged songs of Elvis Presley, who burst on the scene in mid-decade, combining the white gospel and black blues traditions. All these cultural trends marked tensions and stress points in 1950s America that would soon burst into politics and into the streets.

On the political front, President Truman, a feisty underdog in the New Deal tradition, defeated the Republican Thomas Dewey in the 1948 election, but the anti-union Taft-Hartley Act of 1947 signaled a conservative resurgence. Truman's reform proposals, including national health care legislation, made little progress. Dwight Eisenhower's 1952 victory, in tandem with congressional Republicans and conservative Democrats, began eight years of "moderate Republican" rule, which in practice meant accepting the New Deal's basic reforms, while curbing its "excesses."

Cold War anxieties spawned a Red Scare reminiscent of the World War I era. As early as 1947, President Truman instituted a program requiring loyalty oaths of federal employees. Actual espionage cases fed the suspicious climate. In 1948 a former communist, Whittaker Chambers, charged that Alger Hiss, a State Department diplomat, had spied for Russia in the 1930s. Convicted of perjury after investigation by the House Committee on Un-American Activities, Hiss went to prison. In 1950 British authorities arrested Klaus Fuchs, a former Manhattan Project scientist, as a Soviet spy. The unfolding case soon implicated an American couple, Julius and Ethel Rosenberg. Tried and convicted, the Rosenbergs were electrocuted in 1953. In 1954 the Atomic Energy Commission revoked J. Robert Oppenheimer's security clearance on the basis of leftist associations in the 1930s. Hollywood fueled the paranoia with such movies as *I Married a Communist* (1950) and *Invasion of the Body Snatchers* (1956), featuring flesh-devouring aliens masquerading as ordinary citizens. As congressional hearings publicized alleged communist infiltration of Hollywood, radio, and Broadway, performers and artists were blacklisted.

In a 1950 speech in West Virginia, the Wisconsin senator Joseph McCarthy claimed knowledge of several hundred communists in the State Department. Prominent Republicans initially encouraged McCarthy, but as his charges grew wilder (even reaching President Eisenhower), opinion shifted. The end came in 1954, as Arthur Miller's play *The Crucible*, ostensibly about Salem witchcraft, criticized the Red Scare; televised congressional hearings of alleged subversives in the U.S. Army exposed McCarthy's bullying tactics; and a CBS-TV documentary by journalist Edward R. Murrow portrayed McCarthy as a threat to democracy. A Senate censure vote in December confirmed McCarthy's downfall, but "McCarthyism" survives as shorthand for 1950s anticommunist paranoia.

Nuclear fear intensified in the later 1950s as U.S. and Soviet H-bomb tests spread deadly radioactive fallout, and scary civil-defense films taught schoolchildren to "duck and cover." In a surge of activism, U.S. protesters mobilized a test-ban campaign, and writers, artists, and filmmakers addressed the threat. The movie *Them!* (1954), in which giant ants crawl from an atomic test site in New Mexico, launched a flood of mutant movies that tapped into pervasive anxieties. Stanley Kubrick's *Dr. Strangelove* (1963) presented a nuclear apocalypse as black comedy.

In a development of truly historic proportions, the 1950s also brought a major assault on the South's entrenched system of racial segregation. For years, NAACP-sponsored legal challenges had chipped away at the Supreme Court's notorious 1896 ruling upholding segregation. In 1948 President Truman, by executive order, ended segregation in the military. And U.S. racism in its many forms had become a serious Cold War embarrassment as the nation sought friends and allies globally. All this lay in the background in 1954 as the U.S. Supreme Court in *Brown v. Board of Education* (1954) unanimously declared segregated public schools unconstitutional.

The *Brown* decision unleashed long pent-up protest energies, which would transform America. In 1955 Rosa Parks, an officer of the Montgomery, Alabama, NAACP, refused a bus driver's order to move to the back of the bus. Energized by Parks's defiance, African Americans organized a boycott of Montgomery's bus system. Success came in November 1956, when a federal judge ruled all Alabama segregation laws unconstitutional. To lead the boycott, the organizers recruited a young Baptist pastor, Martin Luther King Jr., who soon rose to national leadership of the black freedom struggle and emerged as an authentic American hero, honored with a national holiday.

Southern white racists battled back. In 1957, when Arkansas's governor ordered the National Guard to prevent integration of Little Rock's Central High School, President Eisenhower (though privately critical of the *Brown* ruling) sent in the U.S. Army to enforce the law. Amid these stirring events, Congress passed the Civil Rights Act of 1957, the first federal law challenging racial discrimination since Reconstruction. Shepherded through the Senate by majority leader Lyndon Johnson, a Texas Democrat, and signed by President Eisenhower, this law targeted the stratagems by which southern blacks were barred from voting. Much remained to be accomplished, but this landmark act heralded further victories ahead.

1960–1968: LBJ's "Great Society" and the black freedom struggle

Domestically, the tragically brief Kennedy presidency saw some promising initiatives, but few accomplishments. On November 22, 1963, as he rode in an open car in a motorcade while on a political visit to Dallas, Kennedy was fatally shot by Lee Harvey Oswald. A shocked nation mourned as his body was transported (in a horse-drawn caisson that had earlier carried the assassinated Lincoln) from the White House to the Capitol for memorial services and interred in Arlington National Cemetery.

Newly inaugurated President Lyndon Johnson summoned the nation to fulfill Kennedy's unfinished agenda. And, indeed,

Johnson, a masterful politician, achieved impressive reforms, including his war on poverty, an issue highlighted by Michael Harrington's *The Other America* (1962). The omnibus Economic Opportunity Act of 1964 included funding for jobs training, early childhood education, a domestic volunteer program modeled on the Peace Corps, and anti-poverty initiatives led by local community groups. Poverty rates declined, particularly in black communities. But conservatives soon targeted the program as a chaotic example of governmental overreach.

In a May 1964 commencement address, Johnson offered a vision of national renewal, calling on Americans to build a "Great Society." Congress passed his proposals for public-works projects, rural health centers, urban mass transit, public-education funding, and other reforms. A 1965 immigration act ended the discriminatory quota system. A landmark health-care reform, Medicare and Medicaid, provided medical coverage to older Americans and the poor.

As Rachel Carson's warning of pesticide dangers, *Silent Spring* (1962), stimulated environmental awareness, Congress with LBJ's prodding enacted almost three hundred measures addressing wilderness preservation, air and water pollution, highway beautification, and other concerns. In 1970 millions of Americans observed the first Earth Day to express their commitment to environmental protection.

The civil rights movement, meanwhile, entered a more militant phase. In 1960 four black college students in Greensboro, North Carolina, attended a sit-in at the lunch counter at a local Woolworth store, protesting its refusal to serve blacks. Other activists, black and white, faced violent attacks as they organized "Freedom Rides" challenging segregated southern bus stations. (One black Freedom Rider, John Lewis, brutally beaten in 1961, won election to Congress in 1986.) Newspapers, magazines, and most importantly, television news reports publicized the attacks. Reacting to mounting pressures, President Kennedy created the Equal Employment Opportunity Commission to address job discrimination, and he ordered federal marshals to Montgomery, Alabama, to protect the Freedom Riders, and to the University of Mississippi, where a black man's attempt to enroll provoked deadly riots.

Embodying the new militancy was Malcolm X, born Malcolm Little, who had converted to the Nation of Islam, an African American Islamic movement, in prison. In 1965, challenging the Nation of Islam's leadership as he moved from militant separatism to more inclusive themes of human brotherhood, Malcolm was assassinated by enemies within the movement. Meanwhile, responding to activist pressures, Martin Luther King's Southern Christian Leadership Conference (SCLC) targeted Birmingham, Alabama, for civil rights protests in 1963. As the nation watched, Montgomery police mobilized attack dogs and fire hoses against marching black schoolchildren, and arrested King and other leaders. Tired of bad publicity, the city's white elite eventually agreed to end segregation.

That August, at Washington's Lincoln Memorial, a vast interracial throng celebrated the freedom struggle. Martin Luther King's stirring oration concluded by quoting an African American spiritual, "Free at last. Free at last. Thank God almighty, we're free at last." More violence soon followed, though, including the murder of a Mississippi NAACP official and the bombing of a black church in Birmingham that killed four girls.

But the momentum for change continued. In July 1964, Congress enacted a landmark Civil Rights Act, strengthening the government's power to intervene against voter discrimination and school segregation, and banning racial segregation in the workplace and places of public accommodation such as theaters, restaurants, and motels. A March 1965 demonstration in Selma, Alabama, pitted an increasingly militant SCLC and younger activists against Selma's bigoted sheriff, whose deputies tear-gassed and beat marchers,

11. The March on Washington on August 28, 1963, drew a quarter of a million people to the National Mall. At this high tide of the civil rights movement, they heard Martin Luther King Jr. deliver his memorable "I have a dream" speech in front of the Lincoln Memorial.

again in full view of national television. Protesters poured into Selma and completed a planned march to Montgomery, Alabama's capital. The Voting Rights Act of 1965 soon followed. This measure further strengthened the government's powers to prevent discrimination against black voters. These measures of 1964–65 marked major victories in America's long battle against racism.

Vietnam quagmire: home-front turmoil

As Cold War tensions eased somewhat in Europe and on the nuclear front, Washington's attention turned to Vietnam, a French colony where a communist-led government in the north battled a Western-backed regime in the south. Like Greece in 1947, Vietnam to many Cold War ideologists seemed simply another front in the global struggle between communism and "the Free World." After French withdrawal in 1954, the Eisenhower administration had sent U.S. military advisors to aid South Vietnam's forces; by 1963, they numbered some 16,000. In early November 1963, with U.S. support, a coup by young military officers overthrew and murdered South Vietnam's autocratic ruler Ngo Dinh Diem, a Catholic in a largely Buddhist nation.

Upon taking office, President Johnson initially refrained from full-scale commitment. Indeed, in the 1964 election, Johnson posed as the peace candidate in contrast to the Republican nominee, Arizona senator Barry Goldwater, who frightened voters with talk of all-out war in Vietnam, including nuclear weapons. Ominously, however, in August 1964, Johnson used an ambiguous incident involving U.S. warships in Vietnam's Tonkin Gulf to secure from Congress a sweeping resolution authorizing "all necessary measures" to pursue the war. The Gulf of Tonkin resolution, gloated Johnson, was "like grandma's nightshirt, it covered everything."

Early in 1965, having been elected in a landslide, Johnson announced a major escalation in Vietnam. Defense Secretary

Robert McNamara, Secretary of State Dean Rusk, and other top advisors all concurred. Vietnam, they agreed, represented a test of America's will to battle communism in Asia, Latin America, and Africa—the Cold War's new battlegrounds. They embraced the "domino theory" first propounded by President Eisenhower: if Vietnam fell to communism, surrounding countries would quickly follow.

As Johnson granted General William Westmoreland's never-ending troop requests, the total reached 485,000 by 1967. American bombers rained destruction across Vietnam, "search and destroy" missions sought the elusive enemy, villages considered hostile were burned, jungles were defoliated to expose enemy hiding places. Yet North Vietnam and its South Vietnam allies, the Viet Cong, battled on, and the goal of a stable, anti-communist South Vietnamese government never materialized. As troop morale deteriorated, drug use increased and atrocities occurred. On March 16, 1968, a U.S. platoon murdered more than four hundred men, women, and children in the hamlet of My Lai. After a military cover-up, journalists reported the massacre in 1969. One junior officer was convicted and served three and a half years under house arrest.

As the war dragged on, home-front protests erupted, particularly on college campuses. Students for a Democratic Society, a reform organization founded in 1962, figured prominently in the early antiwar movement. Folk singers Bob Dylan, Joan Baez, and others embraced the antiwar cause. In 1967, several hundred thousand protesters marched in New York City and San Francisco. Defense Secretary McNamara, beset by doubts, resigned that November.

Adding to the crisis atmosphere, rioting and arson hit the black districts of Los Angeles, Newark, Detroit, and other cities in the years between 1965 and 1967. Typically triggered by an incident such as a traffic arrest, the outbreaks revealed deeper frustrations rooted in poverty, joblessness, poor schools, dehumanizing housing projects, and other social problems. Under the mantra "Black Power," some young radicals sought to politicize the seething unrest of the black ghettoes.

Matters reached a crisis in 1968. On January 31, the Vietnamese New Year, a deadly Viet Cong offensive demonstrated its strength across South Vietnam, further weakening support for the war. In March, an antiwar candidate, Minnesota senator Eugene McCarthy (D-MN), defeated Johnson in New Hampshire's Democratic primary. Soon after, Robert Kennedy (D-NY), now a New York senator, entered the race. On March 31 Johnson withdrew from contention.

On April 4, Martin Luther King Jr., now focused on issues of class inequity, systemic northern racism, and the Vietnam War, was assassinated by a gunman in Memphis, Tennessee, where he had come to support striking sanitation workers. National mourning mingled with black riots in several cities that left forty-three dead. On June 5, having just won the California primary, Robert Kennedy was assassinated in Los Angeles. In August, demoralized Democrats nominated Johnson's vice president, Hubert Humphrey, at their Chicago convention. Outside, police brutally attacked war protesters. With political and racial turmoil came cultural conflicts, as many youth, rejecting their elders' lifestyle, embraced rock music, smoked marijuana, let their hair grow, and experimented with LSD and free sex. The Beatles, arriving from England in 1964, won a devoted following. Amplified by media attention, the amorphous "counterculture" contributed to conservatives' worries that society was disintegrating.

Richard Nixon, courting white southerners and America's "silent majority," and pledging an honorable exit from Vietnam, won the Republican nomination. Amid mounting revulsion against campus protests, urban riots, and the counterculture, Nixon narrowly defeated Humphrey, who was fatally identified with

"Johnson's war." A third-party candidate, Alabama's George Wallace, appealed to aggrieved white southerners and blue-collar workers everywhere and won 13 percent of the vote. Nixon and Wallace together swept the once solidly Democratic South, and garnered 56 percent of the vote nationwide, marking a political revolution and a powerful backlash against the course of events since Johnson's 1964 landslide victory.

For all the turmoil and violence, the 1960s also saw the greatest wave of progressive reform since the New Deal, as well as major blows against entrenched racism. Yet more turbulent times lay ahead, and the conservative turn in American public life would continue in the years ahead.

Chapter 9
To the present

Unlike novelists, historians do not have the choice of providing happy endings. Political upheaval, urban violence, and assassinations in the years from 1965 to 1970 launched an era of disorienting change as the United States began its third century of independence. The ensuing decades brought a presidential resignation, a presidential impeachment, a horrific terrorist attack, and contentious foreign wars, culminating in a cycle of rancorous politics and economic recessions. All this unfolded amid disorienting social changes, continuing terrorist fears, long-term anxiety about the nation's economic future, and deepening concerns over global climate change caused by human activity. Despite the Cold War's end and the election of the first black U.S. president—landmark events to be sure—this was hardly America's finest hour. Whether the United States could summon the political will to meet these challenges, and to resolve divisive questions over the role of the state and the balance of individual freedom and the common good, remained uncertain. Yet the nation's history, despite its dark chapters, offered reason for confidence as a troubled future loomed.

A society in transition

While European immigration declined in the later twentieth century, the flow of newcomers from Asia and Latin America surged, as did immigration from India, China, the Philippines, and South Korea. By around 2040, demographers forecast, non-Hispanic whites, long an absolute majority, will comprise fewer than half the total U.S. population. As early as 2003, Hispanics, both legal immigrants and undocumented workers, surpassed African Americans as the nation's largest minority. Defined as those whose native language is Spanish, Hispanics may be of any ethnicity. Mostly from Mexico, the Hispanic population also included Cubans, Puerto Ricans (who are U.S. citizens), and others from Latin America and the Caribbean. Found throughout the labor force, Hispanics worked mostly in agriculture, construction, and human services. Despite their economic contribution, undocumented workers faced punitive legislation and periodic deportation campaigns.

The long-term drop in agricultural employment continued, as giant agribusinesses replaced family farms. Manufacturing declined as other sectors burgeoned: sales; finance; human services; the white-collar professions; and information-technology companies, many in California's Silicon Valley and other areas with a concentration of skilled workers and top educational institutions. As gender discrimination faded, the proportion of women in the workforce rose from 43 percent in 1970 to around 60 percent by 2010.

With the decline of manufacturing, many workers lacking specialized skills faced low-paying jobs with little security and few benefits. Even among the middle class, real income stagnated, and the gap between the super-rich and the rest of society reached levels unseen for many decades. While many blacks and Hispanics achieved middle-class or professional status, others lagged behind, bereft of job prospects and beset by myriad social problems. There was a surge in the number of young black males in prison, mostly for drug-related offenses.

In the United States—and indeed globally—new electronic technologies transformed communications, marketing, and entertainment. Video games and social media enjoyed great popularity. As people went online for news, entertainment, and consumer purchases, book publishers, bookstores, newspapers, magazines, and record companies felt the effects. The spread of big-box retail outlets such as Wal-Mart further transformed the economic landscape, as their ruthless price cutting left shuttered storefronts on many Main Streets.

Amid soaring oil prices and mounting environmental concerns, attention turned at least sporadically to conservation, mass transit, fuel efficiency, and renewable energy. As domestic manufacturing declined, imports of more fuel-efficient automobiles as well as appliances, electronics, and other consumer goods surged, driving up the U.S. trade deficit. With the U.S. economy increasingly enmeshed in a global market, and increasingly hostage to economic crises abroad, and bedeviled by periodic recessions and vast disparities of wealth distribution, the long-term economic prospects looked uncertain at best. Confronted by these unsettling trends, the political system responded fitfully, disrupted by distracting crises and at times seeming nearly dysfunctional.

1969–1980: protests, foreign-policy initiatives, new paths of reform

Elected in 1968, the Republican Richard Nixon promised to end the Vietnam War. Peace talks began in Paris, but under Nixon and his national security advisor (later secretary of state) Henry Kissinger, military aid still flowed to South Vietnam and bombing intensified, including secret raids on Viet Cong strongholds in neighboring Cambodia.

Antiwar demonstrations continued, including massive marches in Washington in 1969 and 1970. On college and university campuses and in San Francisco's Haight-Ashbury district, protest energies took cultural form as well, including the use of marijuana, psychedelic drugs, and the music of the Beatles, Bob Dylan, and others. The counterculture crested in August 1969 as thousands of young people descended on Woodstock, New York, for a three-day rock-music festival and celebration of peace and love. A few protesters turned to violence. In August 1970, explosives planted by four activists at the University of Wisconsin wrecked a campus building housing an army-funded research center, killing a graduate student.

The protests stirred angry opposition, fomented by Alabama governor George Wallace, a 1968 third-party presidential candidate, and by Nixon himself. Blue-collar workers, nicknamed "hardhats," organized pro-Nixon rallies and attacked antiwar demonstrators. On May 4, 1970, Ohio national guardsmen, mobilized by the Republican governor, fired on protesters at Kent State University, killing four and injuring nine. Soon after, police gunfire killed two students at Jackson State College in Mississippi.

In 1971 the *New York Times* published "the Pentagon Papers," a secret Pentagon study making clear the fallacious assumptions underlying the Vietnam War. Antiwar activism faded after 1970. American casualties declined as Nixon withdrew U.S. troops and relied on bombing and the South Vietnamese soldiers instead. The draft ended in 1972, further reducing protests. As the counterculture fragmented, many young people retreated to rural communes, embraced Eastern philosophies, or joined the "Jesus Movement," an amalgam of evangelical piety and the counterculture lifestyle (minus the drugs).

The reformist energies of the 1960s found new outlets. A feminist resurgence, fueled by the National Organization for Women (1966) and Gloria Steinem's *Ms.* magazine (1971), mobilized middle-class women, including veterans of the civil-rights and antiwar movements, to campaign for gender equality and against the culture's underlying patriarchal assumptions. Title IX of a 1972 federal act outlawed gender discrimination in educational hiring and athletics. (Eight years earlier, an amendment to the

Civil Rights Act of 1964, mischievously added by a southern white opponent of the bill, had included "sex" among the categories protected from discrimination.) A June 1969 protest against a police raid on a Manhattan bar frequented by homosexuals launched a gay-and-lesbian rights movement, which would have far-reaching effects. Influenced by Rachel Carson's *Silent Spring,* a new generation mobilized to combat environmental hazards. On April 22, 1970, activists across America observed the first Earth Day. That December, with Nixon's support, Congress created the federal Environmental Protection Agency.

Nixon and Kissinger, meanwhile, focused on foreign affairs. Kissinger's efforts to promote an Israeli-Palestinian peace failed, but his secret overtures to Communist China (Nixon's long-time *bête noire*) bore fruit. In 1972 Nixon and Kissinger met with China's Mao Zedong, laying the groundwork for U.S. diplomatic recognition. Kissinger, a practitioner of balance-of-power diplomacy, also pursued better U.S.-Soviet relations. Closer to home, the administration backed pro-U.S. governments in Latin America and worked to undermine others. In 1973, a U.S.-supported coup in Chile overthrew the democratically elected government of leftist Salvador Allende, who committed suicide. A brutal military junta took power, ruling until 1988.

The election year 1972 found the Democrats split between youthful activists and old-line party stalwarts, including union leaders and big-city politicians. The former, dominating the party convention, nominated South Dakota senator George McGovern, an antiwar leader. Nixon won reelection in a landslide. Pursuing his "Southern strategy," Nixon attracted many traditionally Democratic white southern voters unhappy about black civil-rights gains, as well as blue-collar voters alienated by the Democrats' leftward tilt.

But Nixon soon confronted a crisis of his own making. His well-earned reputation for paranoia and deviousness (encapsulated in the nickname "Tricky Dick") persisted in the White House.

Angered by publication of the "Pentagon Papers," Nixon had authorized a secret team, nicknamed "the plumbers," to investigate leaks. In June 1972, this team broke into the Democratic National Committee's Washington headquarters to install phone taps. A security guard noticed the break-in, and the burglars were arrested. Nixon denied involvement.

The episode initially attracted little notice, but two *Washington Post* reporters pursued the story and secured evidence pointing to White House involvement and subsequent cover-up. A special congressional committee probing the incident soon learned of a secret recording system in the Oval Office. Examination of the tapes revealed Nixon's involvement in concealing the crime. On August 8, 1973, as impeachment loomed, Nixon resigned, the first president to do so. Though he was a man of high intelligence, strategic vision, and shrewd political instincts, Nixon's flawed character ultimately brought him down. Vice President Gerald Ford became president, declaring that "our long national nightmare is over." Ford had been appointed vice president in 1973 when Spiro Agnew resigned that post amid charges of bribery and tax evasion. A likeable if undistinguished Michigan congressman, Ford squandered his initial public goodwill by pardoning Nixon for any crimes committed in office, sparing him from prosecution.

In spring 1975, as Viet Cong troops advanced on Saigon, the last Americans withdrew. The unpopular war finally ended, at a cost of 58,000 G.I.s dead, thousands more wounded, and horrendous Vietnamese casualties. Some believed America could have prevailed if not for home-front opposition; others saw the Vietnam debacle as a monument to U.S. hubris and the risks of allowing ideological abstractions to blur complex geopolitical realities.

Meanwhile, a fresh crisis erupted as Arab states, protesting Washington's support for Israel in a 1973 war, halted oil exports to the United States. As gasoline prices spiked, the national mood soured. With inflation and rising unemployment, domestic auto sales plummeted as buyers turned to more fuel-efficient Japanese imports. With memories of Nixon's perfidy still raw, a Washington outsider, former Georgia governor Jimmy Carter, won the 1976 Democratic presidential nomination and the election, pledging never to lie to the American people. Amid a resurgence of evangelical Protestantism, Carter, a Southern Baptist, proclaimed his faith as a "born-again Christian."

Carter achieved a diplomatic coup in 1978, brokering an Egyptian-Israeli peace treaty. But his domestic record proved disappointing. A technocrat with keen analytic skills, Carter lacked the political touch. As inflation and oil shortages persisted, his popularity plummeted. Dismissing most of his cabinet, Carter called on Americans to conserve limited resources—sound advice, but ill received.

In Iran, meanwhile, Islamic fundamentalists had overthrown the pro-U.S. shah and installed an Islamist regime. In 1979, after Carter admitted the shah to the United States for cancer treatment, Iranian protesters seized the U.S. embassy in Tehran and took sixty-six hostages. This crisis dogged the rest of Carter's presidency. A botched rescue effort cost eight American lives. Only after Carter left office did Iran free the hostages.

The Reagan revolution: conservatism resurgent

Ronald Reagan was a product of Hollywood, where he honed the dramatic skills that served him well in politics. A New Deal Democrat, he moved rightward in the 1950s and became a corporate spokesperson for General Electric. Elected California governor in 1966, Reagan won national attention by denouncing campus protesters. The Moral Majority, a Republican-leaning organization of religious conservatives founded by TV preacher Jerry Falwell, helped Reagan win the 1980 Republican presidential nomination. His sunny optimism and appealing TV persona, combined with Carter's unpopularity, the continuing backlash against 1960s radicalism, and support by religiously conservative voters earned him a landslide victory.

Although evangelical Protestants had been active in the abolitionist movement and other antebellum reforms, they had been largely apolitical thereafter, focusing on church and missionary activities. By the 1970s, however, a host of issues, including abortion, the federal ban on school prayer, the gay rights movement, and a sexually permissive mass media, convinced many evangelicals (as well as conservative Roman Catholics) that the United States was on the wrong path. Falwell's Moral Majority and many other organizations politicized these anxieties, blaming Democratic policies for the nation's moral ills, and evangelicals in massive numbers voted for Reagan in 1980. Ironically, however, Reagan mostly ignored the religious conservatives' cultural agenda, pursuing instead the conservative economic program. Domestically, Reagan called for tax cuts, business deregulation, rolling back environmental-protection laws, opening public lands to private developers, and trimming labor unions' power. When the federal air-traffic controllers went on strike, Reagan fired them. In 1981 Congress enacted a major tax cut and slashed domestic spending. This, Reagan argued, would stimulate the economy and increase revenues. In fact, it eventually produced a recession and soaring deficits. Reagan's sagging popularity revived as the economy improved.

Reagan espoused an individualistic, anti-government, free-market ideology that many found appealing. A gifted communicator, he wrapped his message in a rhetoric of patriotism, nostalgia, and visions of a bright future. While Reagan had fervent supporters, his domestic policies (despite later claims that he was universally beloved) proved deeply contentious.

Pushing big increases in military spending, Reagan stoked Cold War hostilities, labeling the Soviet Union an "evil empire"; U.S.-Soviet relations, already strained owing to Russia's 1979 invasion of Afghanistan, worsened. In this climate, activists organized the so-called nuclear-weapons freeze campaign, pressuring the superpowers to halt nuclear-weapons programs while disarmament negotiations proceeded. As protesters rallied, movies and TV programs warned of nuclear-war dangers. To blunt this movement, Reagan in 1983 proposed his Strategic Defense Initiative (SDI) to develop an impregnable shield against missile attack. Experts dismissed SDI as impractical, and the media labeled it "Star Wars," after a popular science-fiction movie. Nevertheless, Congress funded SDI research, and the freeze campaign faded.

In 1984, with the economy improving, Reagan won reelection. Pursuing its anti-communist agenda, the administration funded insurgents, called contras, battling Nicaragua's leftist government. The administration also sold arms to shadowy groups opposed to Iran's anti-American regime. Defying a congressional ban on U.S. funding of the contras, a National Security Council aide secretly siphoned funds from the Iranian weapons sales to finance the contras. As Congress investigated this crime, Reagan's chief of staff resigned, sparing the president from possible impeachment.

Meanwhile, Cold War tensions dramatically eased as Soviet premier Mikhail Gorbachev, his government under stress at home and abroad, introduced a series of liberalizing reforms. As events spiraled out of control, Eastern Europe slipped from Moscow's grasp and the Communist Party's power in Russia eroded. In this altered climate, Reagan and Gorbachev discussed nuclear disarmament at a conference in Iceland and in 1987 signed a treaty eliminating U.S. and Soviet missiles from Europe. As his term wound down, Reagan, the veteran Cold Warrior, met amicably with Gorbachev in Moscow.

In 1988, Reagan's vice president, George H. W. Bush, won the presidency. A New England patrician turned Texas oilman, politician, and Republican office holder, Bush proved decisive abroad, ineffectual at home. As Russia's hold on Eastern Europe collapsed, symbolized by the 1989 destruction of the Berlin Wall, the Bush administration worked to prevent Russia's nuclear weapons from falling into dangerous hands. A 1991 U.S.-Russian treaty slashed each nation's nuclear arsenals.

With unexpected rapidity, the Cold War had ended. Reagan's admirers credited his hard-line stance for this outcome; others attributed it to internal Russian circumstances. But new dangers loomed in 1990 when the Iraqi dictator Saddam Hussein invaded oil-rich Kuwait. An international coalition assembled by Bush successfully expelled the invaders, but Bush resisted pressures to invade Iraq and overthrow Saddam, judging such a venture too risky. "We stand triumphant," Bush boasted. "We face no enemy menacing our security." His post-Kuwait popularity faded, however, as the administration did little to combat a recession and other domestic economic problems.

The Clinton years: moderation, prosperity, scandal

Bill Clinton, the former governor of Arkansas, won the 1992 Democratic nomination and, with his running mate, Tennessee senator Al Gore, defeated Bush in November. Despite espousing moderate positions targeting independent voters wary of the Democrats' lingering "tax and spend" reputation, Clinton appointed his wife, Hillary Rodham Clinton, to head a task force to propose reforms in America's health-care system. Its sweeping plan for universal health insurance and cost-cutting through purchasing cooperatives and other measures died in Congress amid opposition by physicians, drug companies, and private insurers.

Emboldened by this success, Newt Gingrich, a congressman from Georgia, drafted a "Contract with America" listing Republican policy objectives, including deep spending cuts and measures such as anti-pornography legislation appealing to evangelicals. Republicans regained the House of Representatives in the

1994 midterm elections, and Gingrich became Speaker. But his reputation suffered when failed budget negotiations between Congress and the White House caused a government shut-down.

Clinton, meanwhile, signed a welfare-reform bill that cut welfare spending and reduced Washington's role. Having reclaimed the political center, Clinton won reelection in 1996. His administration's foreign policy achievements included the 1993 ratification of the North American Free Trade Agreement, linking the United States, Canada, and Mexico into a single trading zone, and facilitating a 1995 ceasefire in Bosnia, a part of former Yugoslavia torn by ethno-religious conflict. Scandal marred Clinton's second term as he lied to prosecutors, investigating an earlier sexual-harassment lawsuit, about a sexual relationship with a White House intern. A Republican impeachment effort failed in the Senate, but the episode tarnished Clinton's reputation.

In the 2000 election, Clinton's VP Al Gore opposed Texas governor George W. Bush, son of former president George H. W. Bush. Gore outpolled Bush by more than 500,000 votes, but the Electoral College outcome depended on contested results in Florida. Short-circuiting a recount ordered by the Florida Supreme Court, the U.S. Supreme Court (dominated by Republican appointees) declared Bush the winner. Upon taking office, Bush advocated tax cuts, especially benefitting the wealthy; scaled-back business regulation and environmental-protection measures; and a few reforms favored by his evangelical base. A panel of oil-industry executives convened by Vice President Dick Cheney drafted energy legislation downplaying conservation and extending tax breaks and other benefits to oil and natural-gas companies.

The long shadow of 9/11

On September 11, 2001, terrorists linked to Al Qaeda, a fanatical Islamist organization, hijacked four commercial U.S. passenger aircraft as they took off on domestic flights. Two crashed into the twin towers of New York's World Trade Center, bringing them down. A third hit the Pentagon, and the fourth crashed in Pennsylvania as heroic passengers prevented the hijackers from reaching their target, probably the White House. The attacks killed more than 3,200, including people in the targeted buildings, police and firefighters, and the doomed planes' passengers and crew.

The horrifying assault united the nation and stirred global sympathy. Flag sales soared; the World War II anthem "God Bless America" was revived. Congress passed legislation granting the government sweeping powers to investigate security threats. President Bush pledged a "War on Terror" to "rid the world of evil," targeting Al Qaeda and its leader, Osama bin Laden. U.S. and NATO forces invaded Al Qaeda's stronghold in Afghanistan, ruled by a conservative Islamic movement, the Taliban.

Soon, however, Cheney, the defense secretary Donald Rumsfeld, and others shifted attention to Iraq. Overthrowing Saddam Hussein, they claimed, could make Iraq a beacon of democracy in the Middle East, strengthening Israel's security. Administration figures falsely linked Saddam to 9/11 and insisted that Iraq was secretly building weapons of mass destruction (WMDs).

Barraged by propaganda, Congress approved, and a U.S.-led coalition invaded Iraq in March 2003. Initially the invasion seemed successful. As Saddam and his top henchmen fled Baghdad, Bush proclaimed "Mission Accomplished." (Saddam was eventually captured and hanged.) But sectarian divisions erupted, plunging Iraq into civil war. Home-front disillusionment deepened as no WMDs were found, and journalists documented the deceptive prewar propaganda.

Bush won reelection in 2004, but the war's unpopularity intensified amid reports of atrocities by U.S. troops and torture at military prisons in Iraq and at Guantánamo Bay, Cuba. By 2011, when the U.S. combat role in Iraq finally ended, the toll of American dead stood at 4,484, with more than thirty-three thousand wounded. Iraq, with tremendous casualties from combat and sectarian violence, remained highly unstable. In the view of many, the Iraq invasion represented an appalling misuse of U.S. power.

Historic election; uncertain future

With Bush deeply unpopular, a little-known Democrat, Barack Obama, surged to popularity and won the presidency. Born in Honolulu in 1961 to Ann Dunham, a white U.S. anthropologist, and Barack Obama Sr., a black Kenyan economist, Obama grew up in Hawaii and Indonesia. After graduation from college and work as a community organizer in Chicago, he earned a degree from Harvard Law School, served in the Illinois legislature, and won a U.S. Senate seat in 2004. In 2008 he successfully challenged Hillary Rodham Clinton, by then a New York senator, for the Democratic presidential nomination. (He would later appoint her secretary of state.) A compelling orator, Obama stirred passionate support, aided by his supporters' brilliant use of the Internet and social media, and rode to victory in November—a historic milestone in American life. As Obama noted in his inaugural address, a generation earlier many Washington restaurants would have denied his father service.

But 2008 brought a sharp recession, caused by reckless practices by mortgage lenders, Wall Street securities firms, stock-ratings companies, and lax federal agencies. Stock prices tumbled; productivity stalled; joblessness surged. The federal deficit mushroomed, worsened by Bush-era tax cuts and two unfunded wars. In 2010, after contentious debate, a divided Congress passed a health-care reform bill with provisions to trim costs and extend health insurance to all. Republicans, denouncing "Obamacare" as a socialist plot, gained heavily in the 2010 midterm election. Newly emboldened, they pushed to preserve tax cuts for corporations and the wealthy; further roll back business regulation and environmental protections; and, in the name of fiscal austerity, cut social programs, including Medicare.

The Religious Right pushed its "pro family," anti-gay agenda, and gave rise to a so-called tea party movement (named for the 1773 Boston Tea Party), which exuded suspicion of government and hatred of Obama. As partisan divisions widened, prospects for reasoned solutions to urgent problems faded. With the economy stalled, Republican leaders rejected any stimulus or deficit-reduction proposals involving tax increases, even for the richest Americans. Obama gave ground on issue after issue, fruitlessly seeking compromise with intransigent opponents, and the enthusiasm and passionate hopes he had aroused in 2008 began to fade. Financial crises in Greece and other European nations created fiscal turmoil in the European Union and further slowed U.S. recovery, underscoring the increasingly interdependent nature of the global economy.

12. President Barack Obama presents his economic recovery plan to Congress on September 9, 2009, in the midst of a severe recession. A gifted orator, Obama, like many contemporary politicians, relied on teleprompters, visible on the lectern and to Obama's left.

America's euphoric post–Cold War sense of invulnerability had proven short-lived. Obama refocused military attention on Afghanistan—where outside powers had come to grief for centuries—but conditions remained chaotic. Despite a massive post 9/11 ratcheting up of U.S. security measures, which many feared threatened civil liberties, and even despite the 2011 killing of Osama bin Laden in Pakistan by U.S. special forces, anxiety about terrorist threats remained high.

In 2011, Americans watched with mixed admiration and uneasiness as protesters across North Africa and the Middle East, including long-suppressed Islamist parties, overthrew, or attempted to overthrow, repressive governments, including some, as in Egypt, with close strategic ties to the United States. Efforts to advance Palestinian statehood remained stalled in the face of a hard-line Israeli government and unstable Palestinian leadership, further eroding America's standing in the Arab world.

Across the globe, problems transcending national boundaries cried out for attention, from nuclear proliferation, fossil-fuel depletion, and climate change to poverty, famine, overpopulation, and diseases such as malaria, cholera, HIV/AIDS, pneumonia, hepatitis, and dysentery. Despite many Americans' suspicions of the United Nations and other multinational organizations, their roles seemed certain to expand in the face of urgent transnational challenges.

At home, some Americans foresaw a long cycle of gradual decline, as the economies of China and other emerging markets burgeoned. From a world-historical perspective, such a process would hardly be surprising. Nations and empires rise and fall. Yet the United States over the centuries has shown a capacity for political renewal and creative responses to challenges, with its leadership in the computer and electronic-communications revolutions a recent example. For all its problems, the United States remains a target destination for millions worldwide.

From a still broader perspective, despite setbacks and periods of inertia and reaction, the United States (along with other nations) has proven itself capable of enlarging the realm of freedom, advancing equality and social justice, and promoting the common good. Through political battles and grassroots activism, the nation achieved the expansion of voting rights in the early 1800s; slavery's abolition through a bloody Civil War; corporate regulation, votes for women, and laws protecting consumers and factory workers in the Progressive era; landmark social legislation in the 1930s and the 1960s; and the multiple civil-rights revolutions and environmental-protection measures of more recent times. Thanks to the religious freedom afforded by the First Amendment, the United States has offered a haven for persons of many religious faiths or of none. Despite an early sense of inferiority, Americans have contributed significantly to humanity's achievements in science, medicine, and the creative arts. All this is not to advance some new theory of American exceptionalism, or to deny the many failures, dark passages, and shameful episodes that are also an indelible part of the nation's history. Yet when the balance is drawn, America's record of achievement in advancing human well-being may ultimately outweigh the rest and prove a more lasting measure of national greatness than transient imperial power, military might, or a mere abundance of ephemeral material goods.

References

Chapter 1

James I, "[L]oathsome to the eye," from *A Counter-Blaste to Tobacco* (London: R. B., 1604).

Christopher Columbus, "They ought to make," *The Log of Christopher Columbus*, trans. Robert Fuson (Camden, ME: International Marine Publishing Company, 1991), 77.

Hugh Peters, "You have stepped out of your place," quoted in "Report of the Trial of Mrs. Anne Hutchinson before the Church in Boston," from *The Antinomian Controversy, 1636–1638: A Documentary History*, 2nd ed., ed. David D. Hall (Durham, NC: Duke University Press, 1990), 382–83.

Chapter 2

John Dickinson, "Come join in hand," from "The Liberty Song," quoted in Vera Brodsky Lawrence, *Music for Patriots, Politicians, and Presidents* (New York: Macmillan, 1975), 14–15.

Thomas Paine, "Everything that is right," from *Common Sense*, in *Rights of Man, Common Sense and Other Political Writings*, ed. Mark Philp (New York: Oxford University Press, 2009), 24.

Paine, "The cause of America," from *Common Sense*, in *Rights of Man, Common Sense and Other Political Writings*, ed. Mark Philp (New York: Oxford University Press, 2009), 3.

Paine, "These are the times," from *The Crisis*, in *Rights of Man, Common Sense and Other Political Writings*, ed. Mark Philp (New York: Oxford University Press, 2009), 63.

Abigail Adams, "[R]emember the Ladies," from *The Letters of John and Abigail Adams*, ed. Frank Shuffelton (New York: Penguin, 2004), 148.

George Washington, "[R]ender slavery more irksome," quoted in *This Glorious Struggle: George Washington's Revolutionary War Letters*, ed. Edward G. Lengel (New York: HarperCollins, 2007), 175.

Jehu Grant, "[W]hen I saw liberty poles," quoted in Henry Wiencek, *An Imperfect God: George Washington, His Slaves, and the Creation of America* (New York: Farrar, Straus and Giroux, 2004), 199.

Chapter 3

John Quincy Adams, "[C]ockboat in the wake," from *Memoirs of John Quincy Adams: Comprising Portions of His Diary from 1795 to 1848*, ed. Charles Francis Adams (Philadelphia: J. B. Lippincott, 1875), 179.

Andrew Jackson, "Mr. Marshall has made his decision," quoted in Jon Meacham, *American Lion: Andrew Jackson in the White House* (New York: Random House, 2009), 204.

Andrew Jackson, "[A] few savage hunters," from *Annual Messages, Veto Messages, Protest, &c. of Andrew Jackson*, 2nd ed. (Baltimore: Edward J. Coale, 1835), 59.

Sydney Smith, "Who reads an American book," quoted in Sam Walter Haynes, *Unfinished Revolution: The Early American Republic in a British World* (Charlottesville: University of Virginia Press, 2011), 54.

Oliver Wendell Holmes, "[I]ntellectual declaration of independence," quoted in Peter Gibian, *Oliver Wendell Holmes and the Culture of Conversation* (Cambridge: Cambridge University Press, 2001), 371.

Alexis de Tocqueville, "[T]he most horrific of civil wars," from *Democracy in America*, trans. Gerald Bevan (London: Penguin, 2003), 423.

Chapter 4

Thomas Jefferson, "[A] fire bell in the night," from *The Works of Thomas Jefferson*, vol. 12, ed. Paul Leicester Ford (New York: G. P. Putnam's Sons, 1905), 158.

William Lloyd Garrison, "I will not retreat," quoted in Henry Mayer, *All on Fire: William Lloyd Garrison and the Abolition of Slavery* (New York: W. W. Norton, 1998), 112.

Garrison, "[A]n agreement with hell," quoted in Henry Mayer, *All on Fire: William Lloyd Garrison and the Abolition of Slavery* (New York: W. W. Norton, 1998), 329.

Henry Highland Garnet, "[E]very means," quoted in Fergus M. Bordewich, *Bound for Canaan: The Epic Story of the Underground Railroad, America's First Civil Rights Movement* (New York: HarperCollins, 2005), 227.

John A. Inglis, "[T]he Union subsisting," quoted in Charles P. Roland, *The Confederacy* (Chicago: University of Chicago Press, 1960), 1.

Mary Boykin Chesnut, "We are divorced, North and South," from *Mary Chesnut's Civil War*, ed. C. Vann Woodward (New Haven, CT: Yale University Press, 1981), 25.

Christopher Memminger, "[W]hose opinions and purposes," quoted in Edward McPherson, *The Political History of the United States of America During the Great Rebellion*, 2nd ed. (Washington, DC: Philp and Solomons, 1865), 16.

Chapter 5

William Dean Howells, "The Corliss engine," from "A Sennight at the Centennial," *Atlantic Monthly* 38 (July 1876): 104.

"[W]isest and best citizens," quoted in Mike Wallace and Edwin G. Burrows, *Gotham: A History of New York City to 1898* (New York: Oxford University Press, 1999), 1010.

"When anarchy gathers," from *The Congregationalist*, quoted in Carl N. Degler, *Out of the Past: The Forces That Shaped Modern America* (New York: HarperCollins, 1984), 373.

Richard Olney, "[O]n the ragged edge of anarchy," quoted in Philip Dray, *There Is Power in a Union: The Epic Story of Labor in America* (New York: Anchor, 2011), 204.

Mary Lease, "[R]aise less corn and more hell," quoted in Nancy F. Cott, *Root of Bitterness: Documents of the Social History of American Women* (Boston: Northeastern University Press, 1996), 414.

William Graham Sumner, "A drunkard in the gutter," from *What Social Classes Owe to Each Other* (New York: Harper and Brothers, 1883), 13.

James G. Blaine, "[T]he United States has," quoted in David Saville Muzzey, *James G. Blaine: A Political Idol of Other Days* (New York: Dodd, Mead, 1935), 365.

Walt Whitman, "[T]hen our Republican experiment," from "The Tramp and Strike Questions," *Complete Prose Works* (Philadelphia: David McKay, 1892), 330.

Chapter 6

Upton Sinclair, "I aimed at the public's heart," in *The Profits of Religion: An Essay in Economic Interpretation* (Pasadena, CA: Upton Sinclair, 1918), 194.

Alice Roosevelt, "My father always wanted," quoted in Carol Felsenthal, *Princess Alice: The Life and Times of Alice Roosevelt Longworth* (New York: St. Martin's, 2003), 105.

Chapter 7

John Dos Passos, "All right, we are two nations," from *The Big Money* (New York: Mariner, 2000), 371.

Chapter 8

X [George Kennan], "The Sources of Soviet Conduct," *Foreign Affairs* 25, no. 4 (July 1947): 566–82.

U.S. National Security Council, "[A]nimated by a new fanatic faith," "NSC-68: A Report to the National Security Council, April 14, 1950," *Naval War College Review* (May–June 1975).

Lyndon B. Johnson, "[L]ike grandma's nightshirt," quoted in Robert Dallek, *Lyndon B. Johnson: Portrait of a President* (New York: Oxford University Press, 1999), 179.

Further reading

Preface

Boyer, Paul S., ed. *The Oxford Companion to United States History*. New York: Oxford University Press, 2001.

Cockcroft, James D. *The Hispanic Struggle for Social Justice. The Hispanic Experience in the Americas*. New York: Franklin Watts, 1994.

DuBois, Ellen Carol, and Lynn Dumenil, eds. *Through Women's Eyes: An American History with Documents*. 2nd ed. New York: Bedford/St. Martins, 2008.

Evans, Sara M. *Born for Liberty: A History of Women in America*. New York: Free Press, 1989.

Franklin, John Hope, and Evelyn Higginbotham. *From Slavery to Freedom: A History of African Americans*. 9th ed. New York: McGraw-Hill, 2011.

Herring, George C. *From Colony to Superpower: U.S. Foreign Relations since 1776*. New York: Oxford University Press, 2008.

Jones, Maldwyn A. *American Immigration*. Chicago: University of Chicago Press, 1992.

Chapter 1

Cronon, William. *Changes in the Land: Indians, Colonists, and the Ecology of New England*. Rev. ed. New York: Hill and Wang, 2003.

Elliott, J. H. *Empires of the Atlantic World: Britain and Spain in America, 1492–1830*. New Haven, CT: Yale University Press, 2007.

Mann, Charles C. *1491: New Revelations of the Americas Before Columbus*. New York: Alfred A. Knopf, 2005.

Nash, Gary B. *The Urban Crucible: The Northern Seaports and the Origins of the American Revolution*. Abridged ed. Cambridge, MA: Harvard University Press, 1988.

Richter, Daniel K. *Facing East from Indian Country: A Native History of Early America*. Cambridge, MA: Harvard University Press, 2002.

Chapter 2

Kerber, Linda K. *Women of the Republic: Intellect and Ideology in Revolutionary America*. Chapel Hill: University of North Carolina Press, 1997.

Maier, Pauline. *American Scripture: Making the Declaration of Independence*. New York: Alfred A. Knopf, 1997.

Middlekauff, Robert. *The Glorious Cause: The American Revolution, 1763–1789*. Rev. ed. New York: Oxford University Press, 2005.

Rakove, Jack N. *Original Meanings: Politics and Ideas in the Making of the Constitution*. New York: Alfred A. Knopf, 1996.

Wood, Gordon S. *The Radicalism of the American Revolution*. New York: Alfred A. Knopf, 1993.

Chapter 3

Dublin, Thomas. *Women at Work: The Transformation of Work and Community in Lowell, Massachusetts, 1826–1860*. 2nd ed. New York: Columbia University Press, 1981.

Gura, Philip. *American Transcendentalism: A History*. New York: Hill and Wang, 2008

Heidler, David S., and Jeanne T. Heidler. *The Mexican War*. Westport, CT: Greenwood Press, 2006.

Hickey, Donald R. *The War of 1812: A Short History*. Bicentennial ed. Champaign-Urbana: University of Illinois Press, 2012.

Howe, Daniel Walker. *What Hath God Wrought? The Transformation of America, 1815–1848*. New York: Oxford University Press, 2007.

Wilentz, Sean. *The Rise of American Democracy: Jefferson to Lincoln*. New York: W. W. Norton, 2006.

Wood, Gordon S. *Empire of Liberty: A History of the Early Republic, 1789–1815*. New York: Oxford University Press, 2009.

Chapter 4

Berlin, Ira. *Many Thousands Gone: The First Two Centuries of Slavery in North America*. Cambridge, MA: Harvard University Press, 2000.

Blight, David W. *Race and Reunion: The Civil War in American Memory*. Cambridge, MA: Harvard University Press, 2002.

Faust, Drew Gilpin. *This Republic of Suffering: Death and the American Civil War*. New York: Alfred A. Knopf, 2008.

Foner, Eric, ed. *Our Lincoln: New Perspectives on Lincoln and His World*. New York: W. W. Norton, 2009.

Foner, Eric. *Reconstruction: America's Unfinished Revolution, 1863–1877*. New York: Harper and Row, 1989.

Freehling, William W. *The Road to Disunion*. Vol. 2, *Secessionists Triumphant, 1854–1861*. New York: Oxford University Press, 2007.

Genovese, Eugene. *Roll, Jordan, Roll: The World the Slaves Made*. New York: Pantheon, 1974.

McPherson, James M. *Battle Cry of Freedom: The Civil War Era*. New York: Oxford University Press, 1988.

Chapter 5

Bain, David. *Empire Express: Building the First Transcontinental Railroad*. New York: Viking Books, 1999.

Baker, Jean H. *Votes for Women: The Struggle for Suffrage Revisited*. New York: Oxford University Press, 2002.

Chernow, Ron. *Titan: The Life of John D. Rockefeller Sr*. New York: Random House, 1998.

Pletcher, David M. *The Diplomacy of Involvement: American Economic Expansion Across the Pacific, 1784–1900*. Columbia: University of Missouri Press, 2001.

Pletcher, David M. *The Diplomacy of Trade and Investment: American Economic Expansion in the Hemisphere, 1865–1900*. Columbia: University of Missouri Press, 1998.

Trachtenberg, Alan. *The Incorporation of America: Culture and Society in the Gilded Age*. New York: Hill and Wang, 2007.

Wall, Joseph Frazier. *Andrew Carnegie*. 2nd ed. Pittsburgh: University of Pittsburgh Press, 1989.

Zunz, Olivier. *Making America Corporate, 1879–1920*. Chicago: University of Chicago Press, 1992.

Chapter 6

Diner, Stephen J. *A Very Different Age: Americans of the Progressive Era*. New York: Hill and Wang, 1998.

Kennedy, David M. *Over Here: The First World War and American Society*. New York: Oxford University Press, 1981.

Knock, Thomas J. *To End All Wars: World War I and the Quest for a New World Order*. Princeton, NJ: Princeton University Press, 1995.

Rodgers, Daniel T. *Atlantic Crossings: Social Politics in a Progressive Age*. Cambridge, MA: Harvard University Press, 2000.

Stansell, Christine. *American Moderns: Bohemian New York and the Creation of a New Century*. Princeton, NJ: Princeton University Press, 2009.

Thomas, William H. Jr., *Unsafe for Democracy: World War I and the U.S. Justice Department's Covert Campaign to Suppress Dissent*. Madison: University of Wisconsin Press, 2008.

Chapter 7

Blum, John M. *V Was for Victory: Politics and American Culture during World War II*. New York: Harcourt Brace Jovanovich, 1976.

Dumenil, Lynn. *The Modern Temper: American Culture and Society in the 1920s*. New York: Hill and Wang, 1995.

Hartmann, Susan M. *The Home Front and Beyond: American Women in the 1940s*. Boston: Twayne, 1982.

Kennedy, David M. *Freedom from Fear: The American People in Depression and War, 1929–1945*. New York: Oxford University Press, 1999.

Larson, Edward J. *Summer for the Gods: The Scopes Trial and America's Continuing Debate over Science and Religion*. New York: Basic Books, 2006.

Leuchtenburg, William E. *Franklin D. Roosevelt and the New Deal*. New York: Harper and Row, 1963.

Weinberg, Gerhard. *A World at Arms: A Global History of World War II*. 2nd ed. New York: Cambridge University Press, 2005.

Worster, Donald. *Dust Bowl: The Southern Plains in the 1930s*. New York: Oxford University Press, 1979.

Chapter 8

Andrew, John A. *Lyndon Johnson and the Great Society*. Chicago: Ivan R. Dee, 1998.

Branch, Taylor. *Parting the Waters: America in the King Years, 1954–1963*. New York: Simon and Schuster, 1989.

Evans, Sara M. *Tidal Wave: How Women Changed America at Century's End*. New York: Free Press, 2003.

Gardner, Lloyd C. *Approaching Vietnam: From World War II to Dienbienphu*. New York: W. W. Norton, 1998.

Garrow, David J. *Bearing the Cross: Martin Luther King Jr. and the Southern Christian Leadership Conference*. New York: William Morrow, 1987.

Herring, George C. *America's Longest War: The United States and Vietnam, 1950–1975*. 4th ed. Boston: McGraw-Hill, 2002.

Jackson, Kenneth T. *Crabgrass Frontier: The Suburbanization of the United States*. New York: Oxford University Press, 1986.

Painter, David S. *The Cold War: An International History*. London: Routledge, 1999.

Patterson, James T. *Grand Expectations: The United States, 1945–1974*. New York: Oxford University Press, 1996.

Rosen, Ruth. *The World Split Open: How the Modern Women's Movement Changed America*. New York: Viking, 2000.

Schulman, Bruce J., and Julian Zelizer, eds. *Rightward Bound: Making America Conservative in the 1970s*. Cambridge, MA: Harvard University Press, 2008.

Sitkoff, Harvard. *The Struggle for Black Equality*. 25th anniversary ed. New York: Hill and Wang, 2008.

Chapter 9

Bacevich, Andrew J. *The Limits of Power: The End of American Exceptionalism*. New York: Henry Holt, 2009.

Beschloss, Michael R., and Strobe Talbott. *At the Highest Levels: The Inside Story of the End of the Cold War*. Boston: Little Brown, 1993.

Collins, Robert M. *Transforming America: Politics and Culture during the Reagan Years*. New York: Columbia University Press, 2007.

Ehrenreich, Barbara. *Nickel and Dimed: On (Not) Getting By in America*. New York: Metropolitan Books, 2001.

Hudson, Cheryl, and Gareth Davies, eds. *Ronald Reagan and the 1980s: Perceptions, Policies, Legacies*. New York: Palgrave Macmillan, 2008.

Kolbert, Elizabeth. *Field Notes from a Catastrophe: Man, Nature, and Climate Change*. New York: Bloomsbury, 2006.

Lepore, Jill. *The Whites of Their Eyes: The Tea Party Revolution and the Battle Over American History*. Princeton, NJ: Princeton University Press, 2010.

Maraniss, David. *First in His Class: A Biography of Bill Clinton*. New York: Simon and Schuster, 1995.

McGirr, Lisa. *Suburban Warriors: The Origins of the New American Right*. Princeton, NJ: Princeton University Press, 2001.

Obama, Barack. *Dreams from My Father: A Story of Race and Inheritance*. New York: Times Books, 1995.

Patterson, James T. *Restless Giant: The United States from Watergate to Bush v. Gore*. New York: Oxford University Press, 2009.

Tapscott, Don. *Grown Up Digital: How the Net Generation is Changing Your World*. New York: McGraw-Hill, 2009.

Troy, Gil. *Morning in America: How Ronald Reagan Invented the 1980s*. Princeton, NJ: Princeton University Press, 2007.

Yergin, Daniel. *The Quest: Energy, Security, and the Remaking of the Modern World*. New York: Penguin, 2011.

Index

Page numbers in **bold** indicate illustrations.